VOLUME 3 OF 14 VOLUMES
FRONTIER PRESS COMPANY
COLUMBUS, OHIO

THE LINCOLN LIBRARY OF SPORTS CHAMPIONS

SUSAN BUTCHER, DICK BUTKUS, DICK BUTTON, ROY CAMPANELLA, JOSE CANSECO, JENNIFER CAPRIATI, ROD CAREW, STEVE CARLTON, TRACY CAULKINS, WILT CHAMBERLAIN, BOBBY CLARKE, ROGER CLEMENS, ROBERTO CLEMENTE, TY COBB, SEBASTIAN COE, NADIA COMANECI, MAUREEN CONNOLLY, JIMMY CONNORS, MARGARET COURT, BOB COUSY, LARRY CSONKA.

FIRST EDITION
© SPORTS RESOURCES COMPANY 1974
SECOND EDITION
© SPORTS RESOURCES COMPANY 1978
THIRD EDITION
© THE FRONTIER PRESS COMPANY 1981
FOURTH EDITION
© THE FRONTIER PRESS COMPANY 1985
FIFTH EDITION
© THE FRONTIER PRESS COMPANY 1989
SIXTH EDITION
COPYRIGHT © 1993 BY
THE FRONTIER PRESS COMPANY.
ALL RIGHTS RESERVED UNDER
UNIVERSAL COPYRIGHT AND
PAN AMERICAN CONVENTIONS.
PRINTED IN U.S.A. LIBRARY OF CONGRESS
CATALOG CARD NUMBER 92-75323
ISBN: 0-912168-14-5
NO PART OF THIS WORK MAY BE REPRODUCED
OR USED IN ANY FORM OR BY ANY MEANS,
ELECTRONIC OR MECHANICAL, INCLUDING
PHOTOCOPYING, RECORDING, OR BY ANY
INFORMATION SYSTEM, WITHOUT PERMISSION IN
WRITING FROM THE FRONTIER PRESS COMPANY.

Butcher, Susan (1954-   ),

sled dog racer, was born in Cambridge, Massachusetts. After moving to Alaska in 1975, she raised and trained Alaskan huskies as sled dogs. By 1978, she had developed a dog team that she could race in the Iditarod Trail Sled Dog Race. The race takes place in Alaska and requires drivers and their dogs to travel as fast as they can for days in freezing conditions over a difficult trail. The trail is more than 1000 miles long. Butcher finished 19th in her first Iditarod try in 1978. In 1983 and 1984, she had second-place finishes. But in 1985, a moose ran into her team, causing Butcher

to drop out of the race. That year, Libby Riddles became the first woman to win the Iditarod. Finally, in 1986, Butcher achieved what she had been attempting since 1978. She won the Iditarod. She became the first person ever to win three times in a row when she took first place in the 1988 Iditarod. Butcher won again in 1990, with a record time of 11 days, 1 hour, 53 minutes, and 23 seconds.

Because of several brave teams of sled dogs, the town of Nome, Alaska, was saved. It was in 1925, and the people of Nome were threatened by the terrible disease of diphtheria. They needed the serum that could stop an epidemic of the disease in the crowded, dirty gold-rush town. Some heroic sled dog drivers organized a relay and transported the medicine across the harsh, frozen Alaskan countryside.

By the 1970's, it was the sled dogs who were threatened. The threat was not disease but the increasing popularity of snowmobiles.

Joe Redington, Sr., was one of the people who was worried about the decreasing popularity and importance of sled dogs. He wanted to draw attention to their strength and courage.

Redington helped organize a race that was inspired by the teams who had raced with the lifesaving serum to Nome back in 1925. The race is more than 1000 miles long. Its route is changed slightly from year to year, but it crosses Alaska from Anchorage to Nome. The race was first run in 1973 and is the world's longest dog sled race. Its name is the Iditarod Trail Sled Dog

Race because it roughly follows a trail that was blazed in the early 1900's between the two gold-rush towns of Iditarod and Nome.

The Iditarod helped to bring attention to sled dogs and the people who race them—the mushers. The name *musher* came from the command "mush," which means to start or go faster, although modern mushers often say "hike" or "go." Mushers generally drive teams of from 7 to 18 dogs in a race.

In 1978, a young musher named Susan Butcher competed in her first Iditarod. She had moved to

Alaska in 1975 so she could live with and train sled dogs. Butcher was born December 26, 1954, in Cambridge, Massachusetts, and had loved animals, especially dogs, since her early childhood.

She became a veterinary technician in the early 1970's when she was living in Colorado. While in Colorado, she raced sled dogs for three years. Racing and handling dogs made her dream of moving to Alaska and having her own dogs in a place where mushing could be part of everyday life.

Over the three-year period from 1975 to 1978, Butcher put to-gether her own team made up of Alaskan huskies. These dogs are bred for stamina from lines of old-time Eskimo and Indian dogs.

Butcher's team showed their stamina in their first Iditarod (1978) by helping her win a portion of the prize money. The money is divided among the top 20 finishers. There are usually about 60 competitors in an Iditarod. In subsequent Iditarods, Butcher led her teams to two ninth-place finishes, two fifth-place finishes, and two second-place finishes.

As each Iditarod begins, mushers and their teams leave the start-

Butcher and her dog team cross a frozen lake during the Iditarod.

ing line at two-minute intervals. The dogs are ready to go and must be held back as early teams start out.

Rules of the race require that every racer must stop for a full 24 hours at one of the 24 checkpoints along the trail. Each racer can choose which checkpoint to use for the layover. The enforced rest is important to both dogs and drivers. Sometimes teams will run for eight hours and more without a rest. Often, racers and their dogs will

Butcher, Susan

Butcher runs with her nine-dog team in the finish chute of the 1157-mile Iditarod in 1987. She won the event in 11 days, 2 hours, 5 minutes, and 13 seconds. Susan sliced 13 hours off the course record, a mark she set the previous year.

sleep for only a few hours over a several day period in their attempts to gain the lead.

During an Iditarod, the mushers sometimes cooperate instead of compete so that the race can continue. Because weather conditions can be so terrible along the trail, several drivers will take turns using their teams for the exhausting task of breaking trail.

In 1985, Butcher was sure she could win the grueling race. She had trained her dogs rigorously. Even the best training, however, could not have helped Butcher win or even complete the 1985 race. Just before the fifth checkpoint, Susan and her dogs were racing on a trail through dense forest, and a moose appeared suddenly. The huge animal ran into the team and became entangled in the lines that harness the dog team. The moose stomped two of the dogs to death and injured 13, forcing Susan to drop out of the race.

Still determined to win an Iditarod, Butcher started to plan for the 1986 race. By the end of August in 1985, she was ready to focus on the physical training of her dogs. Before the first snow allowed the use of a sled, the dogs worked out by pulling a wheeled cart.

In February, the month before the Iditarod, racers must complete

the enormous task of gathering over three-quarters of a ton of food and equipment. Then they must arrange to stow a portion of what they will need during the race at each of the 24 checkpoints along the race course. Sleds are fitted with new plastic runner materials, and the dogs are fitted with new harnesses. A thousand dog booties need to be sewn by Butcher and her friends to protect her dogs' paws along the treacherous course.

All the race preparations are expensive, and the prize money helps pay those expenses. The winner's share of the prize money belonged to Susan Butcher for the first time at the end of the 1986 Iditarod. She won the race again in 1987 and 1988, becoming the first person ever to win three Iditarods in a row. When Butcher captured the 1990 race, she broke her 1987 record time and became one of only two competitors to

Butcher and Senator Ted Stevens of Alaska present President Reagan with a sweatshirt commemorating Susan's victory in the 1987 Iditarod.

win a total of four Iditarods.

Susan Butcher was able to become a champion sled dog racer because she inspired her dogs to become champions. Her dogs gave their best efforts because of the many hours she spent with them and because of her great love for all of them.

Butkus, Dick (1942-   ),

football player, was born in Chicago, Illinois. Butkus played fullback at Chicago Vocational High School, where he was an All-America selection. Later at the University of Illinois, as a center-linebacker, he was named as a college All-American in 1963 and 1964. Butkus also led Illinois to its 1964 Rose Bowl victory over the University of Washington. A fierce

tackler and excellent pass-defender, he was chosen in the first round of the college-player draft in 1965 by the Chicago Bears. Dick Butkus was elected as an All-Pro middle linebacker for the next eight years. When he retired following the 1973 season, he held the record for recovered fumbles in the National Football League (NFL), with 25.

Since the days of Bronko Nagurski and Bulldog Turner in the 1930's and 1940's, and on through the time of Ed Sprinkle in the 1940's and early 1950's, the Chicago Bears have been noted for their toughness. They have even been called the "Monsters of the Midway." One of the most fearsome players in Bear history was Richard Marvin Butkus, a 6-foot, 3-inch, 245-pound linebacker. Football seemed to be his whole life. He played it with a force and violence that made him more of a drawing card than the usually more-publicized offensive backfield stars.

Dick Butkus was an all-league choice from his rookie year through 1972. He played all over the field in every game, driving at the quarterback and making hard, jolting tackles. A tribute to his aggressiveness is that he held the National Football League (NFL) record of 25 fumble recoveries when he retired after the 1973 season.

In 1965, Butkus was chosen by the Bears on the first round of the player draft. He had brought terror to the Big Ten for three years at the University of Illinois, where he was an All-American during his last two years. In his rookie year, Butkus intercepted five passes and ran them back for a total of 84 yards. But it was his tackling and desire that won the hearts of the Bears' fans.

Always alert to every action on the field, Butkus was instrumental in a 1971 game that saw the Bears defeat the Washington Redskins in one of the season's most exciting games. In the final seconds of the contest, a bad center snap confused the Bears' kicker, Mac Percival, as he was trying for the extra point after a touchdown. The holder, quarterback Bobby Douglass, retrieved the ball. Then, after a mad scramble, Douglass spotted Butkus waving his arms in the end zone. Promptly, he shot him a 30-yard pass for the point that defeated the Redskins, 16-15.

Dick Butkus had knee surgery after the 1971 season to repair loose ligaments, a condition he had suffered from for 14 years. After the final game of the 1972 season in Oakland, California, a writer asked Gene Upshaw, the Raiders' star

Butkus moves in on the Denver Bronco ball-carrier.

Butkus, Dick

From the time he came into the NFL, Dick Butkus had the reputation as one of football's greatest linebackers.

One of the game's fiercest competitors, Dick waits for the offense to break out of the huddle.

Butkus passed up all other sports as well. He worked out constantly in the off-season on exercises aimed to help him in football.

offensive guard, if he thought Butkus had slipped in ability. Upshaw laughed, "If he has, I'd hate to have met him at his best. He hit me once tonight, and I was out for two minutes."

Born on December 9, 1942, in Chicago, Dick Butkus began playing football early and devoted his teenage years to improving his play. In the eighth grade, he decided he wanted to play pro ball. He entered Chicago Vocational High School, where a Notre Dame graduate, Bernie O'Brien, was the football coach. Butkus had to walk five miles to school. But he did not mind because he felt that O'Brien was the best coach in the area.

The force of his tackles soon became known in football circles, and Butkus had his choice of colleges. He decided on the University of Illinois because it was close to his Chicago home. When he enrolled, Butkus had poor study habits—but Pete Elliott, the head coach, showed him how to knuckle down. The coach convinced Butkus that he needed good grades if he wanted to play football.

While at Illinois, Butkus got married in 1963. That year Illinois won the Big Ten title and went to the Rose Bowl in January 1964.

The University assigned a lawyer to help Butkus in contract talks with the pro teams after his final college season of 1964. In December, he signed with the Chicago Bears for $200,000.

Excited at the prospects of his new pro career, Dick Butkus forgot his diet. When he met the Bears' owner, George Halas, for the first time, his weight had soared to 260 pounds.

"You can be a great linebacker," Halas told his new player, "if you can get down to 245."

A fullback in high school, Butkus shows his skill in running the football after an interception.

Butkus (Number 51) directs the Bear defense.

Butkus, Dick

Butkus (Number 50) and Illinois coach Pete Elliott congratulate each other after the Illini defeated Michigan State in 1963. By virtue of the victory, Illinois clinched the Big Ten title and earned the right to play in the Rose Bowl.

Butkus made no reply, but when he reported to the Bears two months later, his weight scaled at 245 pounds.

Butkus was to contest the post of Bill George, a linebacker for 14 years. But George could not play after an unsuccessful knee operation, so Butkus took over at once. Bubbling over with eagerness, Butkus made many mistakes at first. But he seemed almost impossible to knock down, and he usually bounced back to make the tackle. Then, with every game of every season, Dick Butkus got better and better. He became one of the greatest middle linebackers ever to play the game.

The wear and tear of nine years in the NFL took its toll on Dick Butkus. Injuries prevented him from playing five games in 1973. When the season was over, the meanest "Monster of the Midway" retired. After leaving pro football, Butkus devoted much of his time to acting. He was inducted into the Pro Football Hall of Fame in 1979.

About to tackle Green Bay quarterback Don Horn, Butkus is shown during a 1968 contest.

Dick (Number 51), with a great effort, stops Tommy Mason (Number 20) two yards short of a touchdown.

Butkus brings down Washington Redskin quarterback Bill Kilmer.

13

⛸ **Button, Dick** (1929-),

figure skater, was born in Englewood, New Jersey. He began skating at five, using skates handed down from his brothers. Button started to study figure skating seriously when he was 12. At 14, he won the U.S. novice championship, and the following year he captured the national junior title. At 16, Button was the youngest man ever to win the U.S. senior title, a berth he held for six more years. He changed the style of figure skating with his free movements, adding them to the standard routine. In 1948, Button became the first man ever to win the Grand Slam of skating, taking the U.S., North American, European, Olympic, and world titles in one year. Button won a total of seven national, three North American, one European, two Olympic, and five world figure-skating titles.

With daring jumps and dazzling sit spins, Dick Button became the first American to win an Olympic gold medal in figure skating. A powerful skater in the free-skating competition, Button was the first to include a triple jump in a competitive program. He also popularized the "flying camel"—a jump in which the body and limbs are extended horizontally and the camel position is maintained on landing. Button was also a strong contender in the compulsory (required) figures—the basic skills of figure-skating competition.

In 1948, Dick Button startled the world by sweeping the U.S., North American, European, world, and Olympic championships with a brilliant new style of figure skating.

Until then, Europeans had held all of the international championships and ruled the sport's style. Button's breakthrough ended the European control and changed the major style of free skating for years to come. Before Button's first world performance, the main goal was superior performance in required figures. Free skating was only used as an added display to required skills. Button reversed this tradition.

Figure skating was first added to the Olympic schedule in 1908. But the Winter Games were not added as a separate group of competitions until 1924. The first Winter Olympics were held at Chamonix, a French valley in the Alps, at the base of Mont Blanc. Figure skating was not highly popular in the

United States, and America's teams could not compare with the European competition.

Then, in 1932, Sonja Henie, the champion from Norway, won her second Olympic gold medal at the Winter Games in Lake Placid, New York. From that time on, the popularity of figure skating rose rapidly in America.

Born a few years earlier—on July 18, 1929—in Englewood, New Jersey, Richard Totten Button began his skating career at five. He used a pair of skates handed down from his older brothers, George and Jack.

Button was 12 before he started studying figure skating in earnest. His first teacher said he

would never learn to skate after seeing the 5-foot, 2-inch, 160-pound youth's performance in a neighborhood ice carnival. But young Dick was determined to continue.

Button's parents sent their son to New York City in 1942 to take lessons from skating instructor Joe Carroll. Carroll later took the youngster to Lake Placid, New York, for summer instruction.

At Lake Placid, the young skater soon came under the coaching of Swiss-born Gustave Lussi, a former ski-jumper. Lussi found Button an apt pupil for ideas he had developed about height and length in jumping.

Dick Button's first competition was at the Eastern States championship in New Haven, Connecticut, in 1943. The 13-year-old finished second in the novice division. Button was not pleased. "I want to be first, not second," he declared, and he doubled his training efforts. In the Middle Atlantic championships at New York City in April 1943, Button won his first victory as novice singles champion. Only once again was he a runner-up.

Button attended public grade school in Englewood. Then he went to Englewood School for Boys during his high school years. There he won a letter in football and played baseball. He also continued his grueling schedule on the ice.

Performing a high-flying leap, Button prepares for the 1952 Olympic Games held in Oslo, Norway.

Button worked out 15 to 20 hours a week at first. Then he increased his time to five or six hours a day, starting at 5:30 A.M. so that he could get his school work done.

During the 1943-1944 season, Button joined the Philadelphia Skating Club. He represented the nation's oldest club for all but the last three years of his career, when he competed for the Boston Skating Club.

Button's first U.S. championship came only two years after his first coach had predicted that he would never learn to skate.

Button, Dick

One of the top performers of his day, Button displays his graceful moves during Olympic competition.

Dick Button as a commentator for ABC's Wide World of Sports.

In his third year, 1945, he won the Eastern States senior title at Boston and the national junior championship at Madison Square Garden in New York. He became the first and only person to win the U.S. novice, junior, and senior titles in three straight years when he won the 1946 senior men's title at Chicago. He rallied from second place after the school figures to a unanimous overall victory. Button thus became, at 16, the youngest man ever to win the national senior championship.

He defended this title successfully six straight times, enabling him to represent the U.S. in the 1947 world championships at Stockholm, Sweden—the first international competition since 1939.

Button was runner-up for the second and last time at Stockholm. But the young skater—now 175 pounds on a 5-foot, 10-inch frame —drew wide attention. Because of World War II, Europeans knew little of the progress of American skaters. They were completely unprepared for Button's style. His full-power approach to skating was scorned at first as "acrobatic savagery." But the new stress on jumping was soon widely accepted.

Using every ounce of muscle, Button filled his championship programs with thrilling aerial gymnastics and showy spins. At Stockholm, he first performed the

Button signs an autograph for a youngster during a 1948 stop in New York City after the Olympic Games.

flying camel spin. Within a year, this move was in the program of every competing skater. As leader of the new skating style, Button set a fashion that has since become standard.

The Winter Olympic Games were to be resumed after a pause of 12 years in February 1948, at St. Moritz, Switzerland. Button decided to postpone entering college in the fall of 1947. He planned instead to compete in the European championship events which were scheduled before the Olympics. Button hoped to improve his chances by helping the judges become familiar with his new skating style. His victory at Prague, Czechoslovakia, first and last for an American in the European championships, made him the leading contender for the Olympic Games. It was the last European title for which non-Europeans could compete.

With a panel of judges watching, Button glides over the ice during the men's figure-skating championships at the 1948 Olympics at St. Moritz, Switzerland. Button won the gold medal.

Dick Button went into the free-skating portion of the 1948 Olympics as leader in the school figures. His dazzling program included the first 2½-revolution double Axel jump to be executed successfully in world competition. The jump received a perfect 6.0 mark from one of the judges, and Button won the gold medal.

Two weeks later, in the world championships at Davos, Switzerland, Button became the first Grand Slam skating champion in history. He held the U.S., North American, European, world, and Olympic titles all at once.

A hero's welcome and a White House visit with President Harry Truman greeted Dick Button on his return to the U.S. Later in the year, some 600 sportswriters selected him for the Amateur Athletic Union's James E. Sullivan Award as the year's outstanding amateur athlete. Figure skating had come of age.

Button mixed skating and studies at Harvard University for the next four years. He successfully defended his U.S., North American, and world crowns. He was one of the few representatives of a minor sport to receive a special Harvard "H" for athletics.

Button's career peak came in the 1952 Olympic Games at Oslo, Norway. There, he captured his second gold medal. Including skating's first triple jump (a triple loop) in his program, Button again presented a daring, exciting exhibition. He had mastered the difficult three-revolution feat only six weeks earlier—just as he had perfected the double Axel cleanly only two days before the 1948 Olympics.

In 1952, Button won his fifth world title at Paris and his seventh U.S. senior championship at Colorado Springs. He then returned to Harvard, where he graduated with honors. After 100,000 miles of travel, 15,000 miles of practice, and untold miles of skating, Button retired from amateur competition. He joined the Ice Capades as a guest star during vacations from Harvard Law School.

In 1959, Button led his own troupe on a goodwill tour of the Soviet Union, giving skating exhibitions. In the 1960's, he became known as an expert television commentator covering major skating events.

Other U.S. skaters have since won world championships and Olympic gold medals. But no one has equaled Dick Button's record of seven national, three North American, one European, five world, and two Olympic titles.

⚾ **Campanella, Roy** (1921-   ),

baseball player, was born in Homestead, Pennsylvania, and moved with his family to Philadelphia at an early age. After playing baseball at Simon Gratz High School, Campanella later competed with semi-pro teams in the area. By the time he was 15, he was a professional player with the Baltimore Elite Giants of the Negro National League. He played in Latin America during the winter months. Signed by the Brooklyn Dodgers in 1946, Campanella spent a couple of seasons in the minor leagues before moving up to Brooklyn early in 1948. Playing 10 years as a catcher for the Dodgers, Roy Campanella was named the Most Valuable Player in the National League in 1951, 1953, and 1955. An excellent hitter and defensive catcher,

Campanella helped lead the Dodgers to five National League pennants. In 1958, Campanella was seriously injured in an automobile accident which ended his professional baseball career. The injury was so severe that Campanella was expected to spend the rest of his life in a wheelchair. Roy Campanella was elected to the Baseball Hall of Fame in 1969.

Roy Campanella, elected to baseball's Hall of Fame in 1969, was the backbone of the great Brooklyn Dodger teams of the 1950's. He stands as a model for hard work and a symbol of courage for people everywhere. Battling poverty, injuries, and racial discrimination, Campanella became one of baseball's outstanding catchers.

A professional baseball player from the time he was 15, Roy Campanella spent eight years in the Negro National League before getting his chance at the majors. Once he reached the big-time, he starred for the Dodgers for 10 years. Then, an auto accident cut short his career and confined him to a wheelchair for the rest of his life.

In 1215 major-league games, Campanella batted .276, hit 242 home runs, drove in 856 runs, and had a fielding average of .988. He was also the National League's (NL) Most Valuable Player (MVP) in 1951, 1953, and 1955.

A fine hitter, especially in clutch situations, Campanella was a standout defensive player as well. Although a slow runner, the squatty 5-foot, 9½-inch, 205-pound Campanella was amazingly quick and agile at fielding bunts and pop fouls. He had one of the strongest and most accurate throwing arms in the game. He was also

Campanella tags out New York Giant Jack Harshman at home plate during a battle between the Giants and Dodgers in 1950.

Campanella, Roy

skilled at the most dangerous of all catching jobs—blocking home plate against hard-sliding runners.

Born on November 19, 1921, in Homestead, Pennsylvania, Campanella was the son of a fruit and vegetable salesman. His family moved to Philadelphia early in his youth. Because there was not much money in the household, Roy had to work from the time he was in grade school.

"From the time I was nine or 10, I used to earn my spending money by helping my older brother, Lawrence, deliver milk," recalls Campanella. "I'd get up at 2:30 A.M. to go out on the truck with him and I wouldn't get back to bed until about 5:30 or 6:00. Then I'd have to get up again at 8:00 to go to school. I got a quarter a day for the job."

Campanella's parents often objected to his playing baseball. But nothing could stop him from doing the thing he loved best. Baseball was more than just a source of recreation for him in those early years. It was a way of life. In the beginning, baseball supplied him with the excitement every youngster needs, yet it was not very long before Campanella realized that it could also provide a source of income that the family could use.

Baseball served another purpose for Campanella. He was constantly ridiculed for his roly-poly shape, and baseball was a way of making people take notice of him as an individual. It made him a "somebody."

Campanella's first taste of stardom came at Simon Gratz High School in Philadelphia. But high school ball was not enough to satisfy his desire for competition.

At 13, Roy Campanella was good enough to play for the Nicetown Giants, one of the best semi-pro teams from the Philadelphia area. Roy was now big for his age, had a strong throwing arm, and could hit.

By the time he was 15, his talents were in great demand. He signed to play a few games for the Bacharach Giants, one of the top black semi-pro teams in the area. But he soon left them to play for the Baltimore Elite Giants of the Negro National League.

The Elite Giants paid him $60 a month, a considerable sum for a 16-year-old black youth in 1936. But the fact that he was being paid to play baseball made him ineligible for high school competition. So Campanella quit school after his junior year.

Roy is greeted by the Dodger batboy and Carl Furillo (Number 6) after hitting a home run in the first inning of the third game during the 1955 World Series against the Yankees.

No records were kept of Campanella's achievements in the Negro Leagues. He did well enough, though, to have his salary raised to $90 after the first year and $120 a month after his second year.

In those years Campanella made baseball a year-round occupation. In the winter, when Negro League play was finished, he would travel to Puerto Rico or Cuba to play ball. There, he could earn as much as $45 a week.

"I guess I played about 200 games a year in those days," Campanella remembers. "There were about 125 in the Negro League and about 75 more in Puerto Rico. I usually played ball all but two weeks of the year."

He spent the next five years in the Negro League. Then came the break that enabled him to reach the majors. Campanella had been scouted by the Dodgers during his days in the Negro Leagues. He had even talked to Dodger president Branch Rickey. But he did not know that they were planning to sign him to a big-league contract.

Campanella had dreamed of playing in the majors and would go to big-league games whenever he was not playing himself. On October 23, 1945, his dreams turned into real hopes. The news that day was that Jackie Robinson, a black man, had signed to play for the Brooklyn Dodgers. Baseball's

Campanella, Roy

color barrier had finally been broken.

In a few months, Campanella was signed by the Dodgers. He was assigned to Nashua, New Hampshire, in the New England League in 1946. Assigned with him was another black player, pitcher Don Newcombe, who later starred with the Dodgers. The manager of the Nashua team that year was Walter Alston, who later managed the Dodgers and is ranked as one of the most successful managers in baseball history.

Campanella batted .290 with 13 homers and 96 runs batted in (RBI) for Nashua. Then he was promoted to the Dodgers' number-one farm club at Montreal in 1947. He hit .273 with 13 homers and 75 RBI's at Montreal—which he figured might earn him a spot on the Dodgers for the 1948 season.

He was wrong, but only for a time. The Dodgers sent him to St. Paul in the American Association at the start of the 1948 campaign. But he was recalled promptly at the insistence of Dodger manager Leo Durocher. Campanella played in 83 games for the Dodgers in 1948 and hit nine home runs while batting .258.

The next year, Campanella was the Dodgers' number-one catcher. He hit .287 with 22 home runs and 82 runs batted in and was selected for *The Sporting News*

Roy Campanella and Jackie Robinson —two of baseball's greatest stars—get together for a chat during the spring of 1964. Robinson is showing Campanella his book Baseball Has Done It.

All-Star team. The following year, he improved his statistics to 31 homers, 89 runs batted in, and a .281 batting average.

But it was 1951—the year the Dodgers lost the NL pennant in a dramatic playoff with the New York Giants—that Campanella achieved stardom. That year he batted .325, hit 33 home runs, drove in 108 runs, and led the league's catchers in putouts and assists. He was named the league's Most Valuable Player for the first time.

An injury to his hand caused his batting average and home runs to fall off in 1952. Then he bounced back with 41 homers, 142 runs

batted in, and a .312 average in 1953 to win the MVP trophy again.

Campanella suffered another hand injury in 1954 and endured the worst year of his professional baseball career. He batted just .207 with 19 homers. But, true to form, he rebounded the next year to bat .318 with 32 homers and 107 runs batted in to win his third MVP award.

That was the last good season he had in the majors. By 1956, he

Members of the 1958 Little League World Champions from Monterrey, Mexico, visit Campanella (far right) during his recuperation at New York's Bellevue Hospital.

had slowed down considerably. His statistics for the 1956 and 1957 seasons were hardly up to Campanella standards. Still, when the Dodgers announced in 1957 that they planned to move from Brooklyn to Los Angeles for the 1958 season, Campanella was eager for the new challenge.

Roy Campanella's career came to a sudden end on the morning of January 28, 1958. The car he was driving veered out of control on an icy pavement and crashed. Campanella was pinned underneath the wreckage—his neck was broken, leaving him paralyzed for the rest of his life.

But his great courage and determination pulled him through the hard times, and he adjusted to his new life. That has always been the mark of Roy Campanella. He fights hard because he enjoys life. In his heyday with the Dodgers, his friendly personality and happy-go-lucky attitude were as important to the team as his bat. He remains a man of inspirational qualities.

Campanella receives a standing ovation from baseball dignitaries and fans in 1972 at Los Angeles. Campanella's jersey (Number 39) was retired along with those of Sandy Koufax (in Dodger uniform) and Jackie Robinson (at right with cap).

⚾ Canseco, Jose CAN-SAY-KOH

(1964-   ), baseball player, was born in Havana, Cuba, and grew up in Miami, Florida. Jose did not play baseball until he was 13 and did not make his high school varsity baseball team until his senior year. He was selected by the Oakland A's in the 1982 baseball draft. In his first full year with Oakland, he hit 33 home runs and had 117 runs batted in (RBI). Canseco was named the 1986 American League (AL) Rookie of the Year. In 1988, he led the AL in home runs, with 42, and RBI's, with 124. He also became the first player in history to hit 40 homers and steal 40 bases in the same year. He was named the AL Most Valuable Player (MVP) in 1988. With the

help of Canseco's bat, Oakland won the AL pennant in 1988, 1989, and 1990 and the World Series in 1989. In 1991, Canseco tied for the AL lead in homers, with 44. Toward the end of the 1992 season, he was traded to the Texas Rangers. Blessed with a rare combination of power and speed, Canseco became known for his towering home runs.

He stepped up to the plate, dug his feet into the dirt, and turned his gaze to the pitcher. Jose Canseco now focused everything on the task at hand—to put the ball somewhere in the stands beyond the outfielders' reach.

As he waited, he twitched his neck to the left and then to the right. He arched his back, moved his jaw around, lifted his knee, closed and then opened wide his eyes.

The pitcher leaned back, gath-ered his energy, and threw a blazer straight down the middle. Canseco jumped all over it. With tremendous bat speed, he met the ball chest high and drove it towards center.

Up, up. The center fielder didn't even move—this, he knew, was a lost cause. As Canseco tossed his bat and began his trot around the bases, the ball disappeared into the upper deck beyond the center-field wall.

Fans around the American League (AL) will remember forever the homers they've seen Jose Canseco hit. There was the one in Toronto that hit the window of the restaurant way above center field. And there was the one in Detroit that landed where only one homer had reached before—a legendary smash by Mickey Mantle.

As Jose himself once observed, "Some sluggers just hit home runs. I murder the ball."

Utilizing his awesome strength, Jose Canseco smashes another homer.

Canseco, Jose

Jose Canseco, Jr., was born on July 2, 1964, in Havana, Cuba, along with his twin brother, Osvaldo. Ozzie, as he was nicknamed, was born two minutes ahead of Jose.

The Cansecos had been a well-to-do, highly respected family in Cuba. But a few years before the twins were born, a revolution greatly changed Cuban society. The Cansecos, who opposed these changes, decided to leave the country. When Jose was just nine months old, his parents, he and his brother, and his older sister left Cuba for a new life in Miami, Florida. There, he grew up in the prospering Cuban-American community.

Jose's father had taught English in Cuba, and the Canseco children grew up in their Miami home speaking both English and Spanish. Jose's parents had little interest in sports. They were strict at home and encouraged their children to study hard.

"What I did in school was what mattered to my parents," said Jose. "And I did O.K., too. I was basically an honor student until the 10th grade."

As a kid, Jose played basketball and soccer. He never played on a Little League team—in fact,

Canseco participates in a home-run hitting contest before the 1990 All-Star Game.

Jose (center) celebrates being named the 1986 American League Rookie of the Year with his father, Jose, Sr., and his twin brother, Ozzie.

Jose never even touched a baseball until he was 13 years old.

At Coral Park High School in Miami, both Jose and Ozzie played on the baseball team. Jose had some natural ability, but he was a skinny kid and not outstanding at first. "I didn't even play on the varsity until my senior year," he said.

In that senior year, though, Jose hit .400. The father of one of Jose's friends took notice. That was Camilo Pascual, once a major-leaguer who was then scouting for the Oakland A's. Much to Jose's joy, Oakland selected him in the 1982 baseball draft. As he turned 18, Jose began playing ball for an Oakland minor-league team.

The next year, Jose's twin brother was also drafted by a team, the New York Yankees. Ozzie spent years playing in the minor leagues, as a pitcher and an out-fielder. He eventually played for a while with Jose on the Oakland A's.

Jose also played a few years in the minor leagues, in Idaho, Wisconsin, Oregon, California, Alabama, and Washington. He was a decent fielder and hitter, but showed little greatness.

As a senior in high school, Jose had been a skinny 6-foot, 1-inch, 170-pounder. During his early years in the major leagues, he grew

Canseco, Jose

to become a 6-foot, 3-inch, 240-pound powerhouse.

Jose played some games with Oakland in 1985, but his first full season as a big-leaguer was in 1986. Although he only hit .240 that year, his hits included 33 home runs. Even in batting practice, young Jose was impressive. Fans around the league began showing up early to watch Canseco blast homers before the game. Jose, who also had 117 runs batted in (RBI) that season, was named the 1986 AL Rookie of the Year.

After a good 1987 season, Jose

Canseco clouts his 40th home run of the 1988 season.

and his team had a terrific year in 1988. Canseco batted .307 and led the league in home runs, with 42, and RBI's, with 124. Oakland won the AL pennant before losing to the Los Angeles Dodgers four games to one in the World Series. At season's end, Canseco was named the AL's Most Valuable Player (MVP).

Perhaps even more significant, Jose became the first player in major-league history to hit 40 homers and steal 40 bases in the same season. To do both requires a rare combination of power and speed. Canseco belted the ball like a big man but raced around the bases like a sprinter, making him one of the greatest offensive threats

in baseball history.

"Look at him," remarked teammate Mark McGwire. "He's an awesome physical specimen."

Canseco and fellow power-hitter McGwire became known around the league as the "Bash Brothers." With those two smashing homers and teammate Rickey Henderson stealing bases, the A's won two more AL pennants in 1989

Jose holds up second base after swiping his 40th base of the 1988 season. With his 42 home runs that year, Canseco became the first player in baseball history to collect at least 40 homers and 40 stolen bases in one season.

and 1990—making three straight. Oakland swept the San Francisco Giants in four games in the 1989 World Series. Canseco batted .357 in that Series. In the 1990 World Series, the A's lost to the Cincinnati Reds in four.

By then, Jose had become one of the most popular figures in all of sport. Some fans loved him, and some fans tired of his bragging and irresponsible antics. But everyone noticed him on and off the field.

Jose thrilled crowds with his home runs. One in Toronto landed in the fifth row of the fifth deck. In 1988, he hit three in one game. In 1991, he cracked 44 homers, tying Detroit's Cecil Fielder for the league lead.

Late in the 1992 season, the Oakland A's announced that they were trading Jose. The Texas Rangers would get Canseco; the A's would get All-Star outfielder Ruben Sierra and two pitchers.

Many baseball fans were shocked that Oakland would give up the leading home-run hitter in baseball. In his seven years with the A's, Jose had smacked 231 homers and knocked in 719 runs.

The Texas Rangers and their fans welcomed the talent and excitement that Canseco brought with him. Said Ranger manager Toby Harrah, "You're talking about Jose. He can do it all."

⊖Capriati, Jennifer

CAP-REE-*AH*-TEE (1976-   ), tennis player, was born in Mineola, New York, and spent her first four years with her parents in Spain. The family then moved to Florida. At age four, Jennifer began working with Jimmy Evert, who had coached his daughter Chris to many championships. Jennifer competed in her first tournament at age seven. At age 12, in 1988, she won the girls' 18-and-under U.S. hard-court and clay-court championships. In 1989, she won the Junior French Open and the Junior U.S. Open. In 1990, she turned professional three weeks before her 14th birthday. That year, Capriati was ranked among the top 10 players in the world.

She reached the semifinals of the 1990 French Open and the 1991 U.S. Open. In 1991, she became the youngest-ever semifinalist at Wimbledon. Her first great victory came at the 1992 Olympic Games in Barcelona, Spain, where she won the gold medal in women's singles. Capriati's success came from a sizzling serve and powerful ground strokes.

The players travel from city to city, spending their days on the tennis courts and their nights in hotels. Each seeks fame and fortune on the women's professional tennis circuit. The competition is fierce, and the pressure is tremendous. Parents, coaches, and trainers watch a player's every move and strictly regulate sleep, food, and activity away from the courts.

For teenager Jennifer Capriati, the Olympic village in Barcelona, Spain, proved a refreshing change from the demands of the tennis circuit. The other Olympic athletes were serious about their events but friendly and fun-loving back in the village. "Instead of being with other tennis players," said Jennifer, "you're with all these great athletes. You go for a jog and you have the fastest person in the world passing you."

She hung out with swimmers, rowers, and gymnasts. In the cafeteria, she ate with Bulgarian weightlifters and Japanese judo champions. She played on the beach and set up dates through the village computer system. And she also played the best tennis of her life.

In the 1992 Olympic women's tennis final, Capriati beat Wimbledon champion Steffi Graf in three tough sets, 3-6, 6-3, 6-4. The freedom of the Olympic village was expressed in her free-swinging winners, and Jennifer left Spain with a gold medal around her neck.

Jennifer Capirati established herself as one of the game's top players as soon as she joined the women's tennis tour. She made her pro debut three weeks before her 14th birthday.

Capriati, Jennifer

Jennifer Capriati was born on March 29, 1976, in Mineola, New York, a town on Long Island near New York City. Her father had been a pro soccer goalie in his native Italy and then a movie stuntman in Spain. There, he met Jennifer's mother, an airline attendant. Jennifer's brother, Steven, was born four years later.

Jennifer spent her first few years in Spain. Even as a baby, she showed athletic ability. "Jennifer couldn't have been more than nine months old when I saw her climbing up the monkey bars," recalled her mother. "She couldn't even walk, but she was so strong that she would crawl up to the bars and start climbing."

Her father sometimes taught tennis at a club, and as a toddler Jennifer liked to play around with the balls on the court. By age three and a half, she could hit the balls back and forth across the net.

Not long after, the Capriatis moved to Florida. There, Jennifer's father persuaded tennis pro Jimmy Evert to begin coaching the four-year-old Capriati. At first, Evert balked at the idea. He hadn't begun teaching his own daughter, the great Chris Evert, until she was six. Soon, though, the coach was a believer. "She's the most talented girl I've seen since you," he told Chris.

Jennifer returns volley at the 1992 Olympics in Barcelona, Spain. She won a gold medal in the women's singles competition.

Jennifer played in her first tournament at age seven. By the time she was 10, she was winning 12-and-under tournaments. In 1988, at age 12, she won the girls' 18-and-under U.S. championships on both hard and clay courts. The next year, Jennifer won the Junior French and Junior U.S. opens and also reached the quarterfinals of the Junior Wimbledon.

In 1990, Jennifer, her parents, and her coach decided it was time for her to turn pro. Three weeks before her 14th birthday, she played in her first tournament on the women's circuit. At the Virginia Slims of Florida, she reached the final—the youngest ever to do so—before losing to Gabriela Sabatini. She played well the rest of the year, and she won her first tournament at the Puerto Rico Open.

Capriati's early style was often compared to her friend Chris Evert's. Like Evert, the teenager had a good forehand and a two-handed backhand. But there were differences, partly because Jennifer grew to be 5 feet, 7 inches, and 130 pounds. Her serve was harder and her volleys crisper than Evert's. Retired legend Billie Jean King expressed what most opponents had seen: "Jennifer's got the best ground strokes I've ever seen."

Her game took years to build—and hours daily in practice. As a student at Palmer Academy, a high school for tennis players in Saddlebrook, Florida, Jennifer's schedule was to attend classes about half the day and then put in three or four hours on the court. Weightlifting sessions helped her prevent injury and gave her strokes their fearsome power.

Capriati quickly became one of

the top 10 players in the world. She reached the semifinals of the French Open in 1990. The next year, she became the youngest semifinalist in Wimbledon history. Later that summer, she lost a tough semifinal match to Monica Seles in the U.S. Open. Seles went on to win the final.

Capriati seemed ready to win some major tournaments. But the hardships of the circuit, as well as her growing fame, began to take a toll. She became tired, and she longed for home and her friends. Even at home, though, there were pressures. "When we go shopping," said a friend, "a lot of people ask her for autographs. She doesn't like all the attention."

Not much had gone her way in 1992 until she joined the U.S. team at the Olympic Games. No one gave her much chance to win the gold—except for the swimmers and other athletes whom she had befriended at the Olympic village. Despite never having beaten Steffi Graf before, Jennifer found herself on the medal stand, listening to the national anthem.

"I had chills the whole time," she said. "I just couldn't believe it. I'd watched all the other Americans up there to receive gold medals and I'd say, 'Gee, that would be so cool to be up there.' I got the chance to do what so many other great athletes had done."

⚾ Carew, Rod KUH-*ROO* (1945-   ),

baseball player, was born on a train moving through the Panama Canal Zone. His listed birthplace is Gatun. Carew's family moved to the U.S. when Rod was a teenager and settled in New York City. Signed by the Minnesota Twins, Carew joined the club in 1967. That season, he was selected for the American League (AL) All-Star team at second base and was named Rookie of the Year. Carew won his first batting title in 1969 and, in the same year, tied the major-league records for stolen bases in an inning (3) and most times stealing home in a season (7). He later set a modern-day record with 17 career steals of home. From 1972 through 1975, he was the AL batting champion. He became a first baseman in 1976. With an average of .388 in

1977, Rod took the batting title and was named the AL's Most Valuable Player (MVP). He won his seventh batting crown in 1978. A year later, he was dealt to the California Angels. During his 19 years in the majors, Carew made the All-Star team 18 times. He retired in 1986 with 3053 career hits and a lifetime batting average of .328.

In the 1970's Rod Carew was considered by many the best hitter in the major leagues. Yet for all his skills and batting records, he was one of baseball's "unsung" heroes.

Though respected by his peers, Carew had problems getting the public recognition he deserved during his first 10 years in the big leagues. Part of the reason was that he played for the Minnesota Twins, a team based in an area away from the mainstream of the news media. But some of the reason was Carew himself, who had to fight off the image of a "loner."

Rodney Cline Carew was born on a train passing through the Panama Canal Zone, on October 1, 1945. A sickly child, he grew up in the poverty-ridden section of Gatun, in the Canal Zone. Using rags wound in tape as a ball, Rod began his baseball career.

When Rod was 15, his mother left her husband and moved to New York City. After she found a home and a job, Rod joined her in the U.S.

Rod was sent to George Washington High School in Manhattan. Adjustment to the new surroundings was difficult because his English was poor. And it did not help that he was black and a foreigner.

From 1969 through 1975, Rod Carew won five AL batting titles.

Carew, Rod

Carew cracks a single up the middle.

Finding it difficult to make friends, Rod withdrew into himself. Baseball was his only outlet, although he did not play on the high school team. After school hours, he worked in a grocery store to help support his family.

Eventually, Carew joined a sandlot team, made up mostly of South and Central Americans like himself. It was on the New York sandlots that Rod first caught the attention of Twins' scout Herb Stein. Stein got Rod a tryout at Yankee Stadium. He was so impressive that the Twins signed him to a small bonus contract and sent him to the Rookie League in Melbourne, Florida.

After hitting .325 in 37 games

at Melbourne, Carew moved up to Orlando in the Florida State League in 1965. There, he reached the crossroads of his career.

Rod Carew came very close to quitting professional baseball that year. He was one of the first blacks to play for Orlando, and tension developed between Carew and some of his white teammates. He interpreted certain remarks as racial slurs and nearly quit the team before the season ended. But he was persuaded to finish the season.

The next year, he was sent to Wilson in the Carolina League. More than once during his season at Wilson, Carew threatened to quit. But each time his manager, Vern Morgan, talked him into staying. He finished that season with a .292 batting average.

In 1967, Carew made the big jump to the major leagues, where he again hit .292. He also won the American League's (AL) Rookie-of-the-Year award.

His average slipped to .273 in 1968, but the following season he won his first batting title, hitting .332. From that time, the left-hander did not hit below .300 for 15 years.

He won batting titles from 1972 through 1975, with averages of .318, .350, .364, and .359. He became the first major-leaguer since

In a 1969 playoff game, Carew tags out Baltimore's Brooks Robinson trying to steal second base.

Joe DiMaggio (1939-1941) to bat .350 or better three years in a row. In 1976, he missed a fifth straight title by only .002 percentage points with his .331 batting average.

Rod's batting feats rank him among the game's greats. Only Ty Cobb, Ted Williams, and Wade Boggs ever achieved as many as five AL batting titles, and only Cobb won more in a row.

As a hitter, Carew had no weaknesses. With his exceptionally keen vision, he could tell by the rotation of the pitch whether it was a curve, a fast ball, or a slider. He stood deep in the batter's box so he had a longer time to look at a pitch. He could sometimes even see the ball hit his bat. Rod also had different stances for different pitchers. And when he made contact with the ball, he went with the pitch. If it was inside, he would pull it to right field. If it was outside Rod would spray it to left.

Carew had another weapon in his arsenal—the bunt. He rarely went into a slump, because he was such a good bunter. He legged out a good number of bunts for hits each season. In spring training, he once asked a teammate to throw a sweater onto the infield. He then laid a bunt down on the middle of the sweater. The sweater was moved around the infield, and Rod still rolled them on, one after another.

Yankee manager Billy Martin said of Carew, "Put him in the National League with all those artificial infields, and you've got a .400 hitter with his speed. He's the best hitter in baseball."

Since his early years in professional baseball, Carew had matured greatly. He was still a loner, but the word meant something else now. He was a loner not in the sense that he was always brooding, but because he went his own way.

"When I leave the ballpark,

Carew, Rod

Rod Carew shares the major-league record for most stolen bases in one inning, with three. He accomplished the feat on May 18, 1969.

I'm just Rod Carew—the man going out to enjoy life with my family and friends," he said. "It's only when I get between those two white lines, when I'm out there playing, that I'm Rod Carew the ballplayer."

While he was most famous for his hitting, Carew was by no means a one-dimensional player. He was regarded as one of the best base runners in the game. In fact, Carew tied two major-league records in 1969. He stole three bases in one inning and stole home seven times that season. After playing second base for nine seasons, he was switched to first base in 1976. Carew quickly established himself as one of the best defensive first basemen in the league.

"I'm a complete player," he insisted. "I hit, run, and field. I don't know what more I can do. I always see [read] that I'm just a hitter, not a complete player."

After Carew won his second batting title in 1972, Twins' president Calvin Griffith was reluctant to give his star second baseman a hefty raise—because he was not a home-run hitter. Even after his third straight batting title in 1974, Carew had contract problems with Griffith for the same reason.

So Carew went out to show his owner he could produce runs and still hit for a high average. He drove in 80 runs and hit 14 homers, both career highs, and won his fourth straight batting title with a .359 average in 1975.

Carew bettered his run production in 1976. He drove in 90 runs while stealing a career high of 49 bases.

Then in 1977, everyone noticed Rod Carew. Halfway through the season, he had a batting average of .402. No one in the major leagues had hit .400 in a season since Ted Williams accomplished the feat in 1941. The nation's press began flocking to his door, and Rod's picture appeared on the covers of several national publications.

When the season ended, Carew had won his sixth batting title with a .388 average—the highest mark in many years. He also led the AL in hits (239), runs (128), and triples (16). In addition, he hit 14 homers and 38 doubles, stole 23 bases, and drove in 100 runs. For his remarkable season, Rod was named the AL's Most Valuable Player and *The Sporting News* Major League Player of the Year.

An annual All-Star selection, Carew hit .333 in 1978 to capture his seventh batting championship. In the history of baseball, only Ty Cobb and Honus Wagner had won more batting titles.

Rod Carew retired from baseball in 1986. The year before, he had become the 16th player in history to collect 3000 hits.

In 1991, in his first year of eligibility, Rod Carew was elected to the Baseball Hall of Fame.

⚾Carlton, Steve (1944-   ),

baseball player, was born in Miami, Florida. He attended Miami Dade Junior College, where his baseball skills were noticed by the St. Louis Cardinals. He signed with them in 1964. Carlton helped the Cardinals win two pennants, in 1967 and 1968. In 1969, he set the modern major-league record of 19 strikeouts in a nine-inning game. Shortly before the 1972 season, he was traded to the Philadelphia Phillies. Carlton won 27 games for the Phillies that year, had an earned-run average (ERA) of 1.98, and led the National League (NL) in six pitching categories. His 27 victories stand out because the Phils won only 59 games during the season, finishing in last place. Carlton received the NL Cy Young Award for 1972. He also claimed

the Hickok Belt, presented to the year's top professional athlete. He earned the Cy Young Award again in 1977, 1980, and for a record fourth time in 1982. Steve also helped the Phillies win the 1980 World Series. After 24 seasons, Carlton retired in 1988 with 4136 strikeouts, an ERA of 3.22, and a lifetime won-lost mark of 329-244.

Steve Carlton is proof that the power of "positive thinking" really works. He was a talented, but less than successful, left-hander with the St. Louis Cardinals for five seasons before a try at positive thinking made him one of the best left-handers in the National League (NL) in the 1970's and 1980's.

A 19-game loser with St. Louis in 1970, Carlton took a turnabout in 1971 when he won 20 games for the Cardinals. Traded to the lowly Philadelphia Phillies in 1972, Steve Carlton became the first pitcher in 20 years to win 20 games for a last-place team. He posted a 27-10 record and a 1.98 earned-run average (ERA).

Steve Carlton recorded four more 20-victory seasons. The winningest pitcher in the big leagues from 1974-1983, he was the first hurler to earn four Cy Young Awards. In 1983, "Lefty" became baseball's all-time strikeout leader (later passed by the great Nolan Ryan) and the 16th man in history to post 300 career victories.

Yet, if it had not been for a letter he received from a night watchman in Tucson, Arizona, in

Carlton delivers the ball in his last game of the 1972 season. The Phillies won the game against the Cubs, 11-1. This gave Carlton a season record of 27-10, the best in the major leagues, and a tie with Sandy Koufax for most victories ever by a left-handed pitcher. It was Carlton's 30th complete game of the season—a major-league record. He also had a league-leading ERA of 1.98.

Carlton, Steve

1970, Carlton might never have achieved success as a big-league pitcher. The letter introduced Carlton to positive thinking and told him how to apply it to his work.

The watchman wrote that he was tired of seeing a pitcher of such talent lose.

"He couldn't have been more tired of my losing than me, so I read the letter from beginning to end," Carlton recalls. "He talked in great depth about positive thinking and how it could be applied."

The letters kept coming once a week from the night watchman. And Carlton's entire outlook on pitching changed more with each letter. When he received the first letter in August of 1970, his record was 6-18. From then until the end of the season his record was 4-1.

"The night watchman's letters made me realize that man is the only animal who puts limitation on himself," Carlton says.

Steve Carlton used to worry

about losing. But he learned to get such thoughts out of his mind when he pitched.

"Defeat? I never consider it. Pressure? It doesn't exist. I take every game as it comes. When one ends, I start getting ready for the next one."

Carlton always had the physi-cal ability to be an outstanding pitcher. A lanky 6-foot, 4-inch, 210-pounder, he had a strong arm and excellent command of his three pitches—a blazing fast ball, a slider, and a curve.

Born on December 22, 1944, in Miami, Florida, Steven Norman Carlton spent his entire childhood in Florida, playing baseball at every opportunity. He was playing ball in high school and at Miami Dade Junior College, a school noted for baseball, when he caught the eye of the Cardinals.

The Cardinals signed Carlton in 1964 and sent him to Rock Hill of the West Carolina League,

Carlton, Steve

Steve and Beverly Carlton have a little fun with sons Steven and Scott —a day after Steve's brilliant performance for the St. Louis Cardinals against the New York Mets, September 16, 1969. Carlton set a modern major-league record, striking out 19 batters in a nine-inning game. Even though Carlton passed the mark of 18 strikeouts (once shared by Bob Feller, Sandy Koufax, and Don Wilson), he and the Cardinals lost, 4-3.

where he won 10 of his 11 starts and produced a 1.03 ERA.

After he was promoted to Winnipeg of the Northern League midway through the 1964 season, Carlton was not very effective. He won four games, lost four, and had an ERA of 3.36. Yet, by the sea-

Carlton (right) and the Phillies' general manager, Paul Owens, look over Steve's new contract. It made him the highest-paid pitcher in baseball up to the 1973 season. It was reported that Carlton, who won 27 of the team's 59 games in 1972, was paid $167,000.

son's end, he was pitching with Tulsa of the Texas League.

Carlton made the Cardinals' roster in spring training of 1965 and spent the entire season with them. He was used mostly in relief and pitched only 25 innings, but he struck out 21 batters and had an ERA of 2.52. The Cards decided he needed more work, though, so they sent him back to Tulsa for the 1966 season.

Carlton pitched well enough at Tulsa to be recalled by the Cardinals before the end of the season. By 1967, he was back in the majors to stay.

The Cardinals put Carlton in their starting rotation in 1967, and he helped them win a pennant by posting a 14-9 record. The team repeated as NL champions in 1968, but Carlton's record slumped to 13-11. Then, in 1969, Carlton began to show signs of becoming a truly outstanding pitcher. He won 17 games that year and posted an ERA of 2.17. In one game he set the modern major-league record by striking out 19 batters.

But the next year was a total disaster for Carlton—until he got that letter. He finished the season with a 10-19 record and an ERA of 3.72, but he came into the 1971 season with renewed confidence.

In 1971, he won 20 and lost nine for the Cardinals. But his new-found success caused him to ask for more money in 1972 than St. Louis owner Gussie Busch was willing to pay. Busch settled matters by trading Carlton to the Phillies.

Carlton personally accounted for 46 per cent of Philadelphia's victories that season. Over a two-month stretch, he won 14 straight games and pitched five shutouts. He also led the National League in six major categories—wins (27), ERA (1.98), strikeouts (310), games started (41), complete

Carlton waves to a cheering crowd of 53,377 fans. They have just seen him win his 15th game in a row to become the first 20-game winner in the National League in 1972. Carlton had a spectacular season for the last-place Phillies that year, winning the Cy Young Award.

games (30), and innings pitched (346).

For his outstanding season, Carlton was voted the 1972 Cy Young Award as the NL's top pitcher. He also received the S. Rae Hickok Award as the professional athlete of the year.

The following three seasons were not as rewarding for Steve

Carlton as his stellar 1972 year. In 1973, he slumped badly, winning only 13 games and losing 20. Steve improved his record to 16-13 the next year and led the NL in strikeouts with 240. In 1975, he had an average season, compiling a 15-14 won-lost mark.

Carlton came back in 1976 and pitched superbly. His record of 20-7 helped the Philadelphia Phillies capture the NL East Division title, and his winning percentage topped the league.

Steve had an even better season in 1977. He won 23 games—tops in the major leagues—and lost only 10. His ERA was an im-

pressive 2.64. He again led the Phillies to the NL East title and received his second Cy Young Award.

In 1980, Lefty won his third Cy Young trophy. He posted a record of 24-9 with a 2.34 ERA and a league-leading 286 strikeouts and 304 innings pitched. He also led Philadelphia to victory in the World Series by winning two games against the hard-hitting Kansas City Royals.

Carlton was the only pitcher in the big leagues to reach the 20-victory plateau in 1982. Winning 23 games, he earned an unprecedented fourth Cy Young Award as the NL's best hurler.

Carlton, Steve

Carlton won the Cy Young Award for an unprecedented fourth time in 1982.

Steve's slider plagued NL hitters for many seasons.

As Steve Carlton neared the age of 40, he showed no signs of slowing down. The keys to his durability were his attitude, his great strength, and his wicked slider.

Carlton's positive approach enabled him to ignore distractions and focus his powers of concentration. In his mind, there was no distinction between hitters. There was only himself, the catcher, and the plate. He believed that if he made his pitches, the batter was irrelevant.

To keep his powers of concentration intact, Steve strictly controlled his athletic environment. In the midst of his career, he stopped talking to the press, because he felt that some reporters had treated him unfairly. At the time, he remarked, "I had better things to do after games than spend it with the press. I have just cut all those distractions off."

Carlton became one of the strongest men in baseball. Yet, he did not run or lift weights. The Phillies' strength and flexibility teacher, Gus Hoefling, built Steve's training program around the martial arts. In one exercise, Carlton pushed and

twisted his arms into a deep tub of rice. Former Philadelphia manager Pat Corrales said, "Those exercises are agony—sheer pain. You're talking about 45 minutes of torture."

In the mid-1970's, Lefty mastered the slider, and it became his big pitch. The Carlton slider came in hard, like a fast ball, and appeared to be a strike. But the next thing a hitter knew, "the bottom fell out" and the pitch was in the dirt. Steve's strength enabled him to get

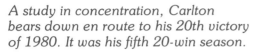

A study in concentration, Carlton bears down en route to his 20th victory of 1980. It was his fifth 20-win season.

a tighter grip on the ball than most men, causing it to break and drop sharply. It was his slider that made his other pitches so successful.

Carlton became the highest-paid pitcher in baseball history with a four-year, $4.15-million pact in 1983. That year, the Phillies won the NL pennant. Steve posted a 2-0 mark and a 0.66 ERA in the NL championship series.

Carlton led the league in strikeouts for the fifth time in 1983. He also became the leading strike-out artist in history. Both he and Nolan Ryan passed Walter Johnson on the all-time list. Philadelphia coach Claude Osteen said, "You hear Ryan's name, and the first thing you think of is strikeouts. But the first thing you think of with Lefty is winning."

In 1983, Steve beat his old team, the Cardinals, for his 300th career victory. On reaching the milestone, he exchanged hugs with his teammates and brought his wife, Beverly, out onto the field. He then retired to a clubhouse closed to reporters.

Steve Carlton ended his career with the San Francisco Giants, Chicago White Sox, Cleveland Indians, and Minnesota Twins. Bound for the Baseball Hall of Fame, the 24-year veteran compiled 4136 strikeouts, an ERA of 3.22, and a record of 329-244.

≈ Caulkins, Tracy (1963-   ),

swimmer, was born in Winona, Minnesota, and grew up in Nashville, Tennessee. By the age of 14, she had mastered all of the competitive swimming strokes. She broke three U.S. records at the Amateur Athletic Union (AAU) Indoor National Championships in 1977. The following year, she became the first woman to swim the 200-yard individual medley in under two minutes. At the 1978 World Aquatic Championships, Tracy won five gold medals and had a part of four world records. She received the Sullivan Award as the nation's top amateur

athlete in 1978. She attended the University of Florida, where she led the swimming team to a National Collegiate Athletic Association (NCAA) title in 1982. That same year, Tracy Caulkins won the 37th national title of her career, surpassing the all-time mark set by the legendary Johnny Weissmuller. At the 1984 Olympic Games in Los Angeles, she won three gold medals.

The East German women's swimming team dominated their sport at the 1976 Olympics in Montreal, Quebec, Canada, winning 11 of 13 gold medals. So it stunned nearly everyone when two years later at the World Aquatic Championships in West Berlin, Germany, the American team roared to an overall victory, smashing the East German squad in the process. Leading the U.S. charge was 15-year-old Tracy Caulkins. She won five gold medals and had a part of four world records.

"She's the greatest woman swimmer that's ever been," said one of her swimming coaches.

Tracy Caulkins was born on January 11, 1963, at Winona, Minnesota. She lived in Iowa before her parents moved the family to Nashville, Tennessee. It was there that eight-year-old Tracy learned to swim.

At first, Tracy would swim only the backstroke—she refused to put her face under water. But soon the pool was her second home. She was ranked nationally by age 10. At 12, she began swimming against major competition. At 14, she startled the swimming world when she broke three U.S. records at the 1977 Amateur Athletic Union (AAU) Indoor National Championships.

"When I first got to the Nationals," Tracy said, "I wondered what I was doing with all these big-time swimmers I'd heard about. Then, I don't know, I just sort of decided I'd like to win."

By the summer of 1978, the 5-foot, 8-inch, 116-pound ninth grader had already set nine U.S. records. She became the first woman to swim the 200-yard individual medley in under two minutes when she swam the event in 1 minute, 59.33 seconds (1:59.33). Tracy's ability to swim all strokes well gave her great advantage in the medley events, which combine laps of backstroke, butterfly, breaststroke, and freestyle.

A few months later, Tracy competed at West Berlin. She set world records in the 200-meter individual medley (2:14.07) and the 400-meter individual medley (4:40.83), and she tied the world record in the 200-meter butterfly (2:09.87). Caulkins and three teammates also set a world record in the 400-meter freestyle relay (3:43.43). She won her fifth gold medal in the 400-meter medley relay.

In recognition, Tracy Caulkins received the 1978 Sullivan Award, given each year to America's outstanding amateur athlete. She was the youngest winner in the award's 49-year history.

Tracy was born with a swimmer's body — tall and sleek with

In 1984, Tracy Caulkins capped her brilliant career by winning three gold medals at the Olympic Games in Los Angeles.

Caulkins, Tracy

long arms and legs. Her knees are able to bend backwards ("hyperextend"), giving her a dolphin-like kick in the water. But without practice, none of that would have made any difference.

From age 12, Tracy would be up six days a week at 5 A.M. to start her workout. In a typical week, she would swim 60 miles and run 11 miles. She would also spend hours lifting weights. Years of conditioning made her a double threat — she had speed for the short races as well as staying power for the long ones.

She spent so much time in

Fifteen-year-old Tracy Caulkins displays the medals she collected at the 1978 World Championships in Berlin.

pools as a youngster that she seemed awkward on dry land. "Tracy is kind of uncoordinated out of the water," kidded her sister Amy, also a swimmer.

Physical abilities alone do not make a champion. Tracy early showed great concentration. She could not be distracted before or during a race. And her dedication inspired her teammates. A coach at the Nashville Aquatic Club, Tracy's home base, said admiringly, "If she were the weakest swimmer on the team, she still would be priceless, she puts out so much."

Tracy set many U.S. and world records, but record times fall quickly in swimming. Her national titles show better how great she became. In 1981, Tracy won her 31st national title, breaking the women's record. The next year, she blew past the all-time record of 36, set by the legendary Johnny Weissmuller more than 50 years before. His were won in eight years and were almost all freestyle titles. She surpassed him in six years, with titles in all strokes.

Caulkins comes up for air during her record-setting performance in the 200-meter breaststroke at the 1980 U.S. Indoor Swimming Championships.

Caulkins makes her final turn and heads to a record-breaking performance in the 400-yard individual medley.

In 1982, Tracy joined the team of the University of Florida. She had grown to 5 feet, 9 inches, and 130 pounds. In her first year at college, she led Florida to the National Collegiate Athletic Association (NCAA) championship.

The U.S. boycott of the 1980 Summer Games had caused Caulkins to miss Olympic competition at the height of her career. She had broken a world record just a few days before the Olympic boycott was announced. In Moscow, she might have won as many as six gold medals. "I suppose I could be over the hill by 1984," she said sadly.

Caulkins was far from being "washed up" in 1984. In preparation for the Olympic Games in Los Angeles, she was put on a rigorous, innovative training program by her college coach, Randy Reese. As part of the grueling routine, Tracy had to swim while harnessed to pulleys and weights.

She warmed up for the Games by winning four individual events at the NCAA Swimming and Diving Championships, adding to her list of NCAA titles. At the U.S. Olympic swimming trials, she was the only triple winner, qualifying for the 200- and 400-meter individual medleys and the 100-meter breaststroke. She also earned a place on the 400-meter medley relay team.

Tracy captured three gold medals at the Olympic Games in Los Angeles. She also set American records in the 200- and 400-meter individual medleys. Since 1977, Caulkins had won 48 national titles and had set 66 world or U.S. records. She had proven herself a great champion.

⊛ Chamberlain, Wilt (1936-),

basketball player, was born in Philadelphia, Pennsylvania. He played college basketball at the University of Kansas, where he led the Jayhawks to the finals of the 1957 National Collegiate Athletic Association (NCAA) tournament. Entering the National Basketball Association (NBA) in 1959 after a year with the Harlem Globetrotters, Chamberlain led the league in scoring for the next seven years. A key player in changing the style of professional basketball, "Wilt the Stilt" was the first 7-footer to play and excel in the pro ranks. In 1967, he led the Philadelphia 76'ers to the NBA title; in 1972, he helped the Los Angeles Lakers to their first championship. Voted the NBA's Most Valuable Player four times, Wilt was the first man to score 30,000 points and the only man to score 100 points in one game. When he left the NBA, he held or shared 43 NBA records, including a single-season scoring average of 50.4. In

14 years, he averaged over 30 points and 20 rebounds a game. For the 1973-1974 season, Wilt jumped to the American Basketball Association (ABA) as player-coach of the San Diego Conquistadors. But he never played in the ABA and retired from basketball just before the 1974-1975 season. Chamberlain was inducted into the Basketball Hall of Fame in 1979.

More than any man in the history of basketball, Wilt Chamberlain was able to bring change to the sport. The era of the tall player began when Chamberlain, 7 feet, 1 inch tall, started playing varsity basketball at the University of Kansas in 1956.

He later became known as the greatest offensive player in the history of pro basketball. He was the first man ever to score 30,000 points in a career. On March 2, 1962, Chamberlain added to his own legend by scoring 100 points in a single pro game, a feat that will

probably never be matched.

That same year, 1962, Chamberlain led the National Basketball Association (NBA) in scoring. He averaged 50.4 points per game—

Chamberlain leaps high over the basket in an effort to grab the ball.

Chamberlain, Wilt

another mark that will be hard to match.

By 1973, Chamberlain held or shared 43 NBA records and had been named the league's Most Valuable Player four times.

Wilton Norman Chamberlain was born August 21, 1936, in Philadelphia, Pennsylvania. His father made a living for the family as a handyman and his mother sometimes worked as a maid. All of the family, including Wilt's six sisters and two brothers, played many kinds of sports.

Of his early success in athletics, Chamberlain says, "I was fast long before I was tall. As early as the third grade, I was running in track and playing football. In the fourth grade in 1946, I made the Penn Relays. I was the anchor spot on the 300-yard shuttle, and my teammates were all sixth-graders. It was quite a big honor.

"Then I began to grow, man, I mean *grow*. One summer before junior high school, I grew four inches over the vacation on my uncle's farm in Virginia, and I came back to Philadelphia about 6 feet tall and a big jumble of wristbones

Dropping out of the University of Kansas, Chamberlain joined the Harlem Globetrotters. Here he is in a Trotter uniform after signing his contract in 1958. Abe Saperstein, the former owner-coach of the Globetrotters, is shown on the left.

Although better known for his basketball skills, Chamberlain is shown here high-jumping 6 feet, 6¾ inches to tie for the 1958 Big Eight Conference indoor championship at Kansas City.

Sailing by former college and pro star Bob Boozer, Wilt coasts in for two points.

Chamberlain, Wilt

and long legs. My mother refused to believe it. 'You're not *my* boy,' she said.''

Chamberlain began practicing basketball with his friends at the YMCA. In 1953, his YMCA team won the U.S. title and Chamberlain was named YMCA All-American.

The Overbrook (Philadelphia) High School basketball team began averaging 120 points per game when Chamberlain played. He became one of the most sought-after players in the history of basketball. Receiving some 200 scholarship offers from colleges, he decided to go to the University of Kansas. There, he was offered a scholarship and a $15-a-week job.

Chamberlain played two varsity years as the nation's scoring sensation at Kansas. A highlight of his college career came in 1957. That year, he led the Kansas Jayhawks into the finals of the National Collegiate Athletic Association (NCAA) tournament. The Jayhawks won hard-fought victories over Southern Methodist University (SMU), Oklahoma City University, and San Francisco State University. But a smaller and less-highly regarded team from the University of North Carolina, coached by Frank McGuire, upset Chamberlain and Kansas in the finals, 54-53, in three overtimes. After

Chamberlain outduels Kareem Abdul-Jabbar and goes up for a two-pointer.

Playing his last season for the Philadelphia 76'ers in 1968, Wilt makes it look easy.

As the fans and his teammates look on in disbelief, Chamberlain goes up to block a Bill Russell shot during the 1969 NBA playoffs.

that game, Chamberlain began to earn a reputation for not being able to win the really big games. Chamberlain dropped out of college during his senior year and joined the Harlem Globetrotters.

Once his college class had graduated, he could be drafted by a National Basketball Association (NBA) team. Chamberlain quit the Globetrotters in 1959 and joined the Philadelphia Warriors of the NBA. Even during his first year, the points never stopped coming from Chamberlain. He led the NBA in scoring for seven straight years until Rick Barry broke the string in the 1966-1967 season. Chamberlain's averages varied from the highs of 50.4 in 1961-1962 and 44.8 in 1962-1963, to a "low" of 34.7 in 1964-1965, the year the Warriors moved to San Francisco. He was always on the All-Star team and was chosen Most Valuable Player four times in the NBA through 1973. The Philadelphia 76'ers paid him a record $250,000 for the 1967-1968 season. Later, he was reported to have signed a

Chamberlain towers over the New York Knicks' Jerry Lucas during the second game of the 1972 NBA playoffs in Los Angeles. The Laker center scored 23 points and grabbed 23 rebounds in the game.

Chamberlain, Wilt

five-year, $3 million contract with the Los Angeles Lakers.

Chamberlain did not get along well with coaches. At least a half-dozen lost their jobs while trying to handle him. Often, the 7-footer was accused of trying to run his own team. Chamberlain disliked practice and often failed to show up. His teammates, as well as the coaches, did not like this because there were things Chamberlain needed to practice. One was foul shooting. His lifetime average at the free-throw line was around 50 per cent. Opposing coaches often considered it good strategy for their players to foul Chamberlain in an effort to stop him.

Chamberlain led the NBA 11 times in rebounding. In the 1960-1961 season, he pulled down a season record of 2149 rebounds. On November 24, 1960, he pulled down a record 55 rebounds for one game.

Until the 1971-1972 season, Chamberlain had played on only one championship team in his career—the 1966-1967 season with the Philadelphia 76'ers. Under the coaching of Alex Hannum, Chamberlain played the best all-round basketball of his career that year. For the first time he excelled on defense, as well as in scoring.

But the years after that went quickly—minus another Cham-

One of the strongest professional athletes in any sport, Chamberlain goes up for a dunk shot against the Phoenix Suns.

Chamberlain enjoyed what he described as his "vindication season." The Lakers, who had failed eight times in the finals, finally won the championship. "He [Chamberlain] was simply the guy who got us there," said the Lakers' backcourt star, Jerry West. Wilt Chamberlain had become a real asset to the defense. His scoring average was only 14.8 that year, the lowest in his career. But Chamberlain played every game and even his critics admitted he had proven he could be a complete player.

After his 14th year in the NBA, Chamberlain jumped to the American Basketball Association (ABA) in 1973. He signed a $1.8-million, three-year contract with the San Diego Conquistadors as player-coach. However, the Lakers obtained a restraining order that barred Wilt from playing in 1973-1974. He coached briefly with San Diego that year and retired from basketball on October 1, 1974.

Chamberlain could have been outstanding in many sports. In his youth, he wanted to be a track star. While playing pro basketball, he developed an interest in volleyball and formed his own team, Wilt's Big Dippers. In 1975, he joined the professional International Volleyball Association. Wilt became the league's president in 1977. But basketball was his first love. He once said, "I love the game—the *pure* game, properly played."

Wilt relaxes with his Great Danes in front of his $1-million estate near Los Angeles, California.

Chamberlain has also made his presence known on the volleyball court. In 1977, Wilt was named president of the International Volleyball Association.

berlain-led championship team in the NBA. Critics were saying, again, that Chamberlain was a jinx to any team with title ambitions. Yet he continued to work hard on defense from 1966 to 1971. His scoring averages dropped into the mid-20's because of it.

But in the 1971-1972 season,

●Clarke, Bobby (1949-),

hockey player, was born in Flin Flon, Manitoba, Canada. He began skating at the age of two and a half and went into junior hockey at 17. Clarke starred in junior hockey for three years and then was the second-round draft choice of the Philadelphia Flyers of the National Hockey League (NHL). What made the play of Clarke so exceptional was that he has diabetes, a disease that requires him to take shots daily. In 1972-1973, Bobby Clarke scored 104 points and won the Hart Trophy as the league's most valuable player. He became the youngest

team captain in NHL history in 1973 and led the Flyers to Stanley Cup championships in 1974 and 1975. Scoring 116 points in 1974-1975 and 119 points in 1975-1976, Clarke led the league in assists both years with 89. Following those two seasons, he received his second and third Hart trophies. Bobby Clarke scored 1210 points during his career.

Bobby Clarke always wanted to be known as something more than a medical curiosity. The reason is simple. When Bobby was 15, doctors found that he had diabetes. To keep the illness under control, he would have to take daily insulin injections and be careful of his diet. Despite his parents' concern about his condition, Bobby continued playing hockey and became the best center in the National Hockey League (NHL).

Robert Earle Clarke was born in Flin Flon, Manitoba, Canada, on August 13, 1949. Flin Flon is a small town in Northwestern Canada, but it has produced many

fine hockey players. Clarke began skating at the age of two and a half when his parents took him to an outdoor ice rink. He started playing hockey when he was eight.

Later, Clarke had the opportunity to play junior hockey. He dropped out of high school at 17 and took a job sweeping floors in a copper mine. His father had spent his life working in zinc and copper mines. "I made up my mind," Bobby later said, "that I wasn't going down into those mines anymore."

His last two years of junior hockey with the Flin Flon Bombers were brilliant—51 goals each sea-

son, 117 assists in 59 games in 1967-1968, and 86 assists in 58 games in 1968-1969.

Clarke's stardom with the Philadelphia Flyers at 23 came as no surprise to Gerry Melnyk, a former NHL forward and scout for the Flyers. Melnyk was the one who sold the Flyer management on drafting Clarke after the left-handed centerman completed his junior hockey career in 1969.

At first the Flyers were not completely sold. They made Clarke

Bobby Clarke's aggressive style of play helped establish him as one of hockey's greatest players.

Clarke, Bobby

Clarke (right) and Boston's Dallas Smith get set to grab the puck.

their second-round choice in the amateur draft in the summer of 1969. Clarke was the 17th player chosen by the NHL teams, behind a host of names that quickly fell into obscurity. The reason Clarke was passed over by so many teams was because of his diabetes.

"I wasn't worried about his diabetes, though," scout Melnyk remembers. "He played 40 to 45 minutes of every game and never stopped working. He had more stamina than any other junior in Western Canada his last year in the juniors. I just couldn't understand how he was passed over so long in the draft."

After the Flyers drafted Clarke, they sent him to the Mayo Clinic in Rochester, Minnesota, for examinations. The doctors there found that a proper diet, especially a big breakfast, in addition to daily insulin shots, could keep Clarke a normal hockey player.

At times, the Flyers have to force Clarke to skip practice to rest for the games. Once they had to keep him in the hospital for an examination so that he would not feel tempted to come to practice. Clarke, self-conscious about his illness, wants no special treatment. "That's not fair to the other guys," he says.

Clarke confessed he did not believe he would make the NHL in his first year out of the junior ranks.

"I really didn't know what to expect," he said. "I thought I'd play in the minor leagues for a while. I told myself I would work hard and, maybe, if I had the talent, I would make it some day."

And make it he did. His play with the Flyers in the early 1970's assured that Clarke would be considered one of hockey's superstars for a long time. In leading the Flyers to a position of respectability in the NHL's West Division, Clarke established a one-season scoring record in 1972-1973 for an expansion-team player. He had 104 points (37 goals, 67 assists), breaking the mark of 82 points (35 goals, 47 assists) set by Red Berenson of the St. Louis Blues in 1968-1969. Clarke's 104 points also made him the second-highest scorer in the league for the year. Also in 1972-1973, Clarke was awarded the Hart Trophy as the league's most valuable player and earned a spot on the NHL's All-Star second team.

The year before (1971-1972),

Team Canada's Bobby Clarke (left) scores his team's second goal during the fifth game in an eight-game series with the Russian national squad. This was the first game of the series played at Moscow in 1972.

Clarke won the Masterton Memorial Trophy as the league player showing the most sportsmanship, hard work, and dedication in hockey.

Clarke was heralded around the world for his fine play even before the 1972-1973 season, his fourth as a professional. As one of the centers for Team Canada in its eight-game series against the Russian national squad in the summer of 1972, Bobby Clarke was one of the stars for his country's team.

Team Canada had to come from behind to capture the series, four victories to three, with one game ending in a tie. Several members of the Russian team, and in particular head coach Boris Kulagrin, declared that in their opinion, Clarke was the best player for Team Canada. He had two goals and four assists in the series.

Elected team captain in January 1973, Clarke had done almost everything for the Flyers—which

surprised no one connected with the team. A fellow Flyer remarked, "When our club is groping and gasping along, Bobby comes to the fore. . . . Leadership isn't walking around before the game, smacking guys on the back. . . . Leadership is making a big play when you really need it. Leadership is Bobby's desire to win."

The following season, 1973-1974, the Flyers were infected with the winning spirit. Led by Clarke's

Clarke, Bobby

Clarke (center) receives the Hart Trophy as the NHL's most valuable player in the 1972-1973 season. He is flanked by former winners Phil Esposito (left) and Bobby Orr (right).

determined and aggressive play, Philadelphia recorded a 50-16-12 mark during the regular season. Bobby scored 87 points, with 35 goals and 52 assists that year. He was selected again for the NHL All-Star second team.

In the Stanley Cup finals of 1974, the Flyers faced Boston. With the Bruins ahead 1-0 in the series, Clarke rose to the occasion in the second game. Philadelphia was behind when Bobby scored his first goal with just a little over a minute gone in the second period. The game ended in a tie and an overtime period—used in the playoffs—followed. Clarke's second goal of the night came in the over-

Bobby Clarke and playoff MVP Bernie Parent carry the Stanley Cup off the ice after their 1974 series victory over the Boston Bruins.

time. It won the game for Philadelphia, 3-2.

The Flyers took the next two games and went on to capture the Stanley Cup championship. They became the first expansion team ever to win it.

On the night of the final victory, the city of Philadelphia celebrated. While car horns blared throughout the night, the sky was lit up by bonfires and endless fireworks. Streakers were everywhere.

The next day, two million people in "the City of Brotherly Love" turned out for the Flyers' victory parade. The wild affair lasted five hours and sent Clarke and some of his teammates fleeing for safety.

In 1974, the Flyers won the Stanley Cup with rough and aggressive play. Many of the opposing teams and fans considered their style "cheap" and "dirty." Clarke, his fellow players, and coach Fred Shero became the center of attention in hockey's controversy over brutality and mindless violence. They were dubbed "the Broad Street Bullies."

On the subject of violence in hockey Clarke said, "Heck, if everyone is really so concerned, they could put in a new rule today that would eliminate the fighting tomorrow. If that's what everybody wants, let's do it. If not, let's get on with the game."

During the 1974-1975 season, Bobby Clarke and the Flyers were again superb. Bobby scored 116 points, led the league in assists with 89, and was awarded his second Hart Trophy.

Before the playoffs, Clarke approached Philadelphia goalie Bernie Parent and said, "Look, you're the one guy who can win the Stanley Cup for us. Do it and I'll buy you a jeep." And for the second year in a row, the Flyers captured the Stanley Cup—and Parent repeated as the most valuable player in the playoffs. Bobby Clarke delivered the jeep.

Clarke also delivered in the playoffs. He tied for the lead in assists with 12, and scored a goal and an assist in the second game of the final series against the Buffalo Sabres. The Flyers won that game, 2-1.

The next year, Clarke kept his reputation as the hardest working player in the NHL. Again, he led the league in assists (89) and tied for the lead in assists (14) during the Cup playoffs. Bobby scored 119 points and added a third Hart Trophy to his collection.

He became a playing assistant coach for Philadelphia before the 1979-1980 season. The Flyers established an NHL record by playing 35 games without a loss en route to

Bobby Clarke was considered the hardest working player in the NHL.

the 1980 Stanley Cup finals.

Bobby Clarke gave everything he had—and more. He could do it all. He scored when the team needed it the most; he dogged opponents with his forechecking; he killed penalties; he was devastating on power plays; and he won most of his face-offs. It seemed he was everywhere and at just the right time.

Clarke retired in 1984 with 358 goals and 852 assists. He then

served as general manager of the Flyers and the Minnesota North Stars and as senior vice president of the Flyers. He was elected to the Hockey Hall of Fame in 1987.

As a competitor, Bobby Clarke was called "mean" and "the dirtiest player in the league." Others praised him as the game's "superstar." Off the ice, he was called "an amazing human being" and a "once-in-a-lifetime guy." To all of these compliments and criticisms, Clarke responded, "Aaw, naaw, none of that stuff is true."

⚾ Clemens, Roger (1962-),

baseball player, was born in Dayton, Ohio, and moved to Houston, Texas, in high school. He practiced pitching endlessly, and great control was his reward. Nolan Ryan was the young pitcher's idol. Roger pitched the University of Texas to victory in the final game of the 1983 College World Series. He was drafted that June by the Boston Red Sox. Following a brief stint in the minor leagues, Clemens joined the Red Sox. In his first two seasons, 1984 and 1985, he was plagued with injuries. In 1986, Clemens became the first man in baseball history to strike out 20 batters in a nine-inning game. He then earned Most-Valuable-Player (MVP) honors in the All-Star Game. Roger posted a 24-4 record and a 2.48 earned-run average

(ERA) in 1986, leading Boston into the World Series. That year, he won both the Cy Young Award and the MVP award in the American League (AL). He won 20 games in 1987 and earned his second straight Cy Young Award as the league's best pitcher. Clemens topped the circuit with a 1.93 ERA in 1990 while posting a 21-6 record. He won the AL Cy Young Award again in 1991.

It took 111 seasons. Finally, someone struck out 20 batters in a nine-inning baseball game.

On April 29, 1986, Roger "the Rocket" Clemens of the Boston Red Sox achieved the record by zipping a 97 mile-per-hour fast ball past Phil Bradley of the Seattle Mariners. Clemens broke the all-time mark held by Steve Carlton, Tom Seaver, and Roger's hero, Nolan Ryan, without giving up a single walk. He struck out the side in the first inning, the fourth, and the fifth. He won the three-hit masterpiece, 3-1.

"I've seen perfect games by Catfish Hunter and Mike Witt, and I've seen some great games pitched by Seaver," said Red Sox manager John McNamara. "But I've never seen a pitching performance as awesome as that, and I don't think you will again in the history of baseball."

For future generations, the Baseball Hall of Fame asked for the glove, spikes, and cap Clemens wore during the game, as well as for the ball he threw past Bradley for strikeout number 20. "I'm in the Hall of Fame," exclaimed Roger. "That's something nobody can take away from me."

Clemens won the Cy Young Award as the AL's top pitcher in 1986, 1987, and 1991. In 1986, he also was named the league's MVP.

Clemens, Roger

Rookie Roger Clemens posts his first big-league victory against the Minnesota Twins in 1984.

William Roger Clemens was born August 4, 1962, in Dayton, Ohio. He was a standout pitcher in Little League. In high school, he moved to Texas. Roger wasn't considered the best pitcher on his high school team, but he believed in his ability. He worked hard — he lifted weights, did calisthenics, and ran every day.

As a teenager, Clemens attended Astros games and rooted for his idol, Nolan Ryan. "He threw hard — put fear into batters — and I wanted to be just like him," said Roger. Clemens also liked Ryan's mechanics, especially the way he used his legs to drive off the mound to the plate during his delivery.

Roger was obsessed with his own pitching motion. He practiced his delivery in front of a mirror every day. Unlike the young Nolan Ryan, the young Roger Clemens

developed masterful control of his pitches.

The New York Mets picked Roger in the 12th round of the 1981 amateur draft. He ended up not signing with the team. (If he had signed with the Mets, he would have been in the same pitching rotation with Mets' ace Dwight Gooden!) Clemens enrolled at the University of Texas instead.

After pitching Texas to the College World Series championship, Roger was drafted by the Red Sox in 1983. He made a quick trip through the minor leagues. He played only 18 games. His earned-run averages (ERA) of 1.24, 1.38, and 1.93 on three different levels of minor-league play rocketed him into the big leagues.

Clemens poses with the game ball after striking out 20 Seattle Mariners in a 1986 game. The mark set a major-league record.

In 1984, as a member of the Red Sox, Clemens was being compared to Dwight Gooden. But when Roger pulled a muscle in his right forearm, it ended his season. The next year, he began to suffer severe pain in his right shoulder. He was forced to miss a big chunk of 1985.

Not many people knew how much Roger's life was affected by not being able to pitch. Those days were full of agony, frustration, and fear for the 6-foot, 4-inch, 220-pound right-hander. His career was in jeopardy.

Clemens underwent arthroscopic surgery to remove a fragment of cartilage around the rotator cuff of his pitching arm in August of 1985. A day after the operation, he was doing weight exercises.

Roger was a new man in 1986. He won 14 straight games to begin the season — the fifth best start by a pitcher in baseball history. One of those games was his 20-strikeout performance against the Mariners. In that contest, he tied the American League (AL) record for consecutive strikeouts (8). Roger delivered his blazing fast ball with pinpoint accuracy.

"Rocket was unhittable," said Boston's catcher Rich Gedman after the game. "The thing that amazed me the most was that the Mariners had so many swings and weren't even able to foul the ball."

Power pitcher Roger Clemens notches another strikeout.

Clemens was beside himself. "I'm going to savor every moment, sign every autograph." And to think that only eight months before that big game, a shoulder operation threatened to end Roger's career.

Chosen as the starting pitcher in the 1986 All-Star Game, Clemens earned Most-Valuable-Player (MVP) honors. He worked three innings — retired the National League (NL) lineup in order — and earned the victory.

Clemens finished the 1986 season with a record of 24-4 and an ERA of 2.48. Both statistics topped the league. Fourteen of his victories came after Red Sox losses. He totaled 238 strikeouts. Roger's efforts led Boston into the World Series, where they lost to the New York Mets in a thrilling seven-game battle.

Consolation for Clemens came

later when he was named winner of both the Cy Young Award and the MVP honor in the American League. He was also chosen as the Major League Player of the Year by *The Sporting News.*

In 1987, Clemens was unhappy with the contract he was offered and boycotted most of spring training. He didn't perform well at the beginning of the regular season. He finished strong, however, throwing back-to-back shutouts to end the season.

Clemens led the majors with seven shutouts and 18 complete games, and he tied for the lead in victories. His record was 20-9. His 2.97 ERA was third best in the league, and he ranked second in strikeouts with 256. Again, Roger won the Cy Young Award, becoming the first back-to-back winner since Jim Palmer in 1975 and 1976.

In 1988, Roger posted 18 wins and league-leading totals for shutouts (8) and strikeouts (291). He won 17 games in 1989.

Clemens' rigorous regimen of sprints, distance running, and the use of free weights and aerobic machines helped keep him at the top of his game. He practiced on a pitcher's mound he built at his home, based on the measurements of the mound at Boston's Fenway Park. He also kept a book on hitters and umpires.

Clemens, Roger

As a mature pitcher, Clemens continued to rely on his renowned fast ball. He had one grip to make his fast ball spin backward and rise, and another grip to make it spin like an auger (a tool for boring holes) and sink. He also developed an effective curve ball, fork ball, and slider.

In Roger's mind, he had to face three major situations in a game. First, he had to shut the other team down and gain momentum for his club. Then, he had to expect to have a stretch where he was forced to pitch out of at least one jam. Finally, he had to close the game.

Judging by his 1990 season, Roger came to the ballpark well prepared. He was 21-6 with a league-leading 1.93 ERA. If he had not missed a handful of starts in September, he might have won another Cy Young Award. Before the next season, 1991, the Red Sox made Clemens the first player in baseball history to earn $5 million a year.

Clemens received his third Cy Young Award in 1991. He compiled an 18-10 record, and he led the league in strikeouts (241), shutouts (4), and ERA (2.62). Roger's importance to his team was monumental in 1991. Eliminate Roger from the Red Sox rotation and Boston starters were 47-51 with a 4.83 ERA.

In 1992, Clemens won 18 games, and he again led the league

Clemens gets ready to unleash a mighty fast ball.

Restrained by catcher Tony Pena, Clemens argues with umpires after getting ejected from Game 1 of the 1990 American League Championship Series. Roger was tossed out of the game for challenging calls made by home-plate umpire Terry Cooney.

in ERA (2.41) and shutouts (5). He became the first AL pitcher since Lefty Grove to lead the league in ERA three seasons in a row.

From 1986 through 1992, Roger recorded at least 200 strikeouts every season. And in those seven years, his 136 total victories and 2.66 ERA were the best marks in the major leagues.

Roger Clemens was asked once by a reporter if he felt any pressure to perform at such a high level each time he stepped on the mound. He responded, "Pressure? From the time I was in Little League, I always wanted to be where it was all on the line."

⚾ Clemente, Roberto

CLEH-*MEN*-TEE (1934-1972), baseball player, was born in Carolina, Puerto Rico. He played only softball until he was 17, then signed with a professional baseball team in Puerto Rico. Three years later, he was noticed by the Brooklyn Dodgers, signed for a bonus, and shipped to their Montreal farm club. From Montreal he was picked up by the Pittsburgh Pirates. He played with the Pirates for 18 years, until his death in a plane crash on New Year's Eve, 1972. Roberto Clemente collected 3000 hits in major-league play, which puts him in a select group. Elected to the All-Star team 12 times, he won four National League batting titles and received the Gold Glove award 11 times. In 1966, Clemente was voted the Most Valuable Player (MVP) in the league, and in 1971 he received

Most-Valuable-Player honors in the World Series. In that Series he collected 12 hits, including two home runs, for a .414 average. By the time of his death, Clemente was one of the greatest baseball players of all time. A special election was held 11 weeks after Roberto Clemente's death, and he was voted into the Baseball Hall of Fame.

The record books are filled with the feats of Roberto Clemente of the Pittsburgh Pirates. Yet, figures tell only part of the story of this man who was known as "The Great One" in his native Puerto Rico.

Rated as one of the finest outfielders and hitters to play major-league baseball, Clemente collected 3000 hits and compiled a .318 batting average in 18 big-league seasons before his death in an airplane crash on New Year's Eve, 1972.

During his career he had more hits and drove in more runs than any other Pittsburgh player before him. He won four National League batting titles: 1961, .351; 1964, .339; 1965, .329; 1967, .357. In 1966, Clemente was selected as the league's Most Valuable Player (MVP) after hitting .317 and knocking in 119 runs.

Clemente's fielding skills matched his batting skills. He won the Gold Glove award for his work in right field 11 times. Five times he led the National League in throwing out base runners from the outfield.

The great Clemente—waiting in the on-deck circle.

Clemente, Roberto

Probably the three finest players of their day—Henry Aaron, Willie Mays, and Clemente.

Perhaps his greatest performance came in 1971. At the age of 37, he led the Pirates to victory over Baltimore in the World Series. In the Series, Clemente had 12 hits—with two home runs, two doubles, and a triple—and batted .414. He played brilliantly in the field and ran the bases with speed and daring. For his efforts he was voted the outstanding player in the World Series.

Roberto Walker Clemente was born on August 18, 1934, in Carolina, Puerto Rico. His father was a foreman at a sugar cane plantation and his mother ran a grocery store and meat market for the plantation workers. Their hard work left a strong mark on young Roberto.

Clemente did not play baseball until he was 17 years old. He was a softball player when he was noticed by the owner of the Santurce Cangrejeros, a Puerto Rican pro baseball team.

Clemente spent three seasons with Santurce. In his third year, he was seen by a scout from the Brooklyn Dodgers of the National League. The Dodgers signed him to a contract, with a $10,000 bonus. The rules at that time stated that any player signed for more than $4000 had to be placed directly on the major-league team or he could be drafted by another club. The Dodgers did not feel Clemente was

Clemente slaps a base-hit against the Baltimore Orioles in the 1971 World Series. The Pirate star had an outstanding series, batting .414, being voted the Most Valuable Player, and leading Pittsburgh to the world championship.

Making a beautiful slide, Roberto steals second base.

Clemente, Roberto

Clemente leaps high into air, making a valiant attempt to snare a San Francisco Giant home run.

ready for the majors, but they did not want to lose him. They sent him to their Montreal, Canada, farm team. The Dodgers did not want anyone to see how good Clemente really was, and as a result he played very little. But Clyde Sukeforth, a scout for the Pittsburgh Pirates, noticed him. Sukeforth at once urged the Pirates to take him as their first choice in the player draft.

The Pirates drafted Clemente for $4000. The Dodgers not only lost one of the game's great players, but also $6000 at the same time.

For his first five years, Clemente was not a first-rate hitter. But, from 1960 to 1972, he batted under .300 only once, reaching a high of .357 in 1967.

As a player, few could equal him for all-round talent. He was a muscular 5 feet, 11 inches tall and weighed 185 pounds. He had a powerful throwing arm, superb running speed, and lightning-quick reflexes.

"He was the greatest all-round player during my era," said Bill Virdon, who played with Clemente and later was his manager. "He could do more things than anybody I've ever seen."

He had an unusual batting style and was a hitter who studied each pitcher with care. "The very special thing about Roberto, physically, is his hands," said Tom

A pitcher's nightmare—Roberto Clemente in the batter's box.

One of the finest defensive outfielders ever to play the game, Clemente outdid himself on this play. Slipping in the muddy outfield, he was still able to hang on to the ball.

Clemente, Roberto

Clemente stands on second base (at far left of picture) after he became one of 11 players in major-league history to get 3000 or more hits. The hit, which came on September 30, 1972, was his last in regular-season play. It came only three months before he was killed in a tragic airplane crash.

Pittsburgh Pirates' manager Bill Virdon points to the special patch that was worn in 1973 on the left shoulder of the Pirate uniforms in memory of Roberto Clemente. The black 21 was Clemente's uniform number.

Clemente takes time out to visit with his wife, Vera, and three sons, Enrico (in his father's arms), Roberto, Jr. (center), and Luis, before a game against the New York Mets.

Roberto signs autographs for his enthusiastic fans.

Seaver, who pitched against Clemente often. "So very powerful. He stood there far away from the plate with that great big long bat, and with those strong hands he controlled it like crazy, hitting pitches on the side of the plate."

Of Clemente's fielding talents, Frank Robinson said, "Watching him move to his left to grab the ball and then turning to his right to fire it was really something to see. There aren't many ballplayers who could do it."

Clemente's skills on the baseball diamond were never questioned. But as a person he was not always understood. He often complained of his injuries. He believed in his skills, and throughout his career, he complained that reporters were unfair in their treatment of Latin American players, himself included. In 1960, for ex-

ample, the Pirates won the National League pennant, and shortstop Dick Groat was elected as the league's Most Valuable Player. Clemente, who hit .314 that year and drove in 94 runs, felt he should have been named the MVP. When the Pirates won the World Series, Clemente would not wear his championship ring. Yet, he was always friendly to his teammates and the fans.

Clemente was a folk hero in his native Puerto Rico. He was always eager to help others with his time, money, and energy. On the night his plane crashed off the coast of Puerto Rico, he was on his way to deliver supplies to survivors of an earthquake in Nicaragua.

His private life centered on his work of helping others, and on his wife, Vera, and three sons. In his last season with the Pirates, he was one of baseball's highest-paid

After Clemente's death, Pittsburgh bid farewell to its favorite son as the bright lights of the ALCOA message board towered over the city. The message, in Clemente's native Spanish, translates as "GOODBYE FRIEND ROBERTO."

players at a yearly salary of $150,000.

Normally, a player must be out of the game five years or more before he is eligible for the Baseball Hall of Fame in Cooperstown, New York. Yet, just 11 weeks after Roberto Clemente's death, a special election was held and he was voted into the Baseball Hall of Fame.

Clemente's feats on the field will live as long as there are people interested in baseball. But the people of Puerto Rico will remember him longer for the helping hand he was always ready to lend.

⚾ Cobb, Ty (1886-1961),

baseball player, was born in Narrows, Georgia. He took part in baseball as a youngster and later played on two minor-league teams in the South. Cobb signed with the Detroit Tigers when he was 19 and stayed with them for 22 of his 24 seasons in the major leagues. One of the game's greatest hitters, he led the American League in batting 12 times and had a lifetime batting

average of .367. He also batted over .400 three seasons, led the league in 12 offensive categories in 1911, and paced the Tigers to three American League pennants. Feared and respected on the base paths, Cobb stole a record 892 bases in his career—96 of them in one season. Ty Cobb was the first player selected for the Baseball Hall of Fame.

When the Baseball Hall of Fame in Cooperstown, New York, was opened in 1939, the first memento placed in the museum was a pair of baseball shoes with long spikes. "That takes care of Ty Cobb," said one of the judges, "now let's see who else belongs."

Known as the "Georgia Peach," Cobb was hailed by many as baseball's greatest star, and was rated as its fiercest competitor.

Of his 24 years in the major leagues, 22 were spent with the Detroit Tigers. Ty Cobb played in 3033 games, scored 2244 runs, and collected 4191 hits. His lifetime batting average was an incredible .367. And he led the American League in batting 12 times.

Cobb was a great hitter, runner, and base stealer. He stole 892 bases in his career, a record that was not broken until 1977.

Cobb played for 22 years with the Detroit Tigers, and then for two years with the Philadelphia Athletics. When he retired in 1928 at the age of 42, he had set 16 major-league records.

Cobb was also the first player inducted into the Baseball Hall of Fame in Cooperstown, New York. He polled 222 out of 226 votes to lead the first five all-time stars selected for the Hall in 1936.

Tyrus Raymond Cobb was born in Narrows, Georgia, December 18, 1886. He was the oldest son in a distinguished and wealthy family. His father, W. H. Cobb, was

a state senator.

Ty Cobb was introduced to baseball by a Methodist minister named John Yarborough. Yarborough coached a team of youngsters —the Royston (Georgia) Midgets— and recognized Cobb's unusual talent right away. Before long, Ty became a member of the team.

Cobb did not grow up wanting to be a baseball player. As a boy he wanted to become a surgeon, but his father wanted him to be a lawyer. Father and son argued hotly over which career young Ty would go into. Cobb saw baseball as a way out of these arguments with his father.

He began writing letters to baseball teams, asking to try out.

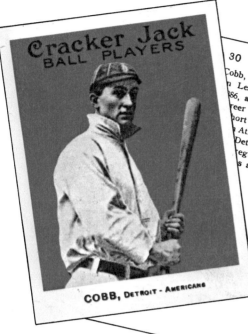

Cracker Jack
BALL PLAYERS

30

Cobb, center fielder of
League team, was
86, at Royston, Ga.
reer began in 1904,
hort time with the
Atlantic League.
Detroit in 1905.
egular member
a marvel for

COBB, Detroit - Americans

This Ty Cobb baseball card was one
of a series of color pictures of famous
ballplayers and managers given free
with Cracker Jack early in the 20th
century.

Cobb playing the outfield for the
Philadelphia Athletics during the 1927
season.

Cobb, Ty

When he got no answers, he asked Reverend Yarborough for help. Yarborough helped Cobb make the Augusta, Georgia, team in the South Atlantic (Sally) League. When Cobb's father found out about it, he almost disowned his son. In those days, professional baseball players were looked upon as tramps. It was shocking for a person of Cobb's social class even to consider a career in baseball. After some urging from Reverend Yarborough, Cobb's father finally agreed to let his son play on the Augusta team.

An outstanding hitter and daring runner, the 6-foot, ¾-inch, 175-pound Cobb became a fiery, bull-headed, and brilliant player.

The Detroit Tigers had their first look at him when the team was at spring training in Augusta. At that time, Cobb made a nuisance of himself at the Tiger practice games. That year, though, Cobb was the star player of the South Atlantic League. Glowing reports of his play began coming in to the Detroit office, so the Tiger manager sent a scout to watch the 18-year-old play. Cobb was out of action with an injury the day he arrived, but the scout decided to take a chance on him. The Tigers got young Cobb from Augusta for between $700 and $750, probably the greatest bargain in baseball history.

In those days, rookies were always hazed by the older players. There was no exception when Cobb joined the Tigers. They remembered Cobb as the cocky kid from spring training, and they played practical jokes on him, knotting his clothes, breaking his bats, and other tricks. But the harder they were on Cobb, the more he fought back. "The hazing I got from those men made me mad," Cobb once said. "I was just a kid and I vowed I'd show 'em. I resented the rough, tough way they acted. I soon found the manners my family had taught me had no place in baseball. I decided I'd forget about being a gentleman and be tougher and

Cobb's plaque hangs at the Baseball Hall of Fame at Cooperstown, New York.

Here is one of baseball's greatest action pictures—showing Ty Cobb sliding into third base in 1909. Before his career ended, Cobb stole 892 bases.

Cobb, Ty

meaner than any of them." Cobb liked to fight. He was not well liked by his teammates, and opposing players feared him. But his fierce desire to win helped make him the best player of his time.

After hitting only .240 in his rookie season, Cobb batted over .300 for 23 straight seasons. Three times he hit over .400, and in the 1911 season he set the American League records for runs, hits, doubles, triples, extra-base hits, total bases, runs batted in, and stolen bases.

Cobb could hit a bad ball as well as a good one, if a hit was needed. It was when the opposing team was at its roughest, and hostile crowds rode him hardest, that he rose to his greatest heights as a player.

Cobb dominated every game he played, and sometimes he got into fights with fans and players. His dazzling running and base stealing upset enemy pitchers and threw enemy outfielders off their game. One manager once asked his catcher, "What do you do when Cobb breaks for second?" The catcher replied, "I throw to third!" Several times Cobb stole second, third, and home in one inning.

Cobb was his own toughest critic and taskmaster. He studied every type of batting form and mastered them all. His advice to young players was, "Work at what doesn't

Ty took time out to sign a few autographs for his young admirers at San Francisco, California, in 1920.

come easy to you."

Cobb played for three American League pennant-winners. Despite his great success as a player, he was never as popular as such later stars as **Babe Ruth**, **Lou Gehrig**, and **Willie Mays**. Cobb's angry attitude made more enemies than friends.

Ty Cobb's holdings in General Motors and Coca-Cola during his playing days made him a millionaire in later years. After he retired from baseball, he lived a life of leisure in

This George "Honey Boy" Evans Champion Baseball Trophy was presented to Ty Cobb after he won the 1912 American League batting championship with a .410 mark.

Atherton, California. Even in retirement he managed to complain about present-day ballplayers. But, despite his grumblings about the national game, he still kept a great interest in the sport until his death in 1961.

Cobb signs a 1927 contract with the Philadelphia Athletics. The great Connie Mack (right) looks on with A's executive Tom Shibe.

⏱ Coe, Sebastian

(1956-   ), distance runner, was born in London, England. He began running cross-country as a teenager. His father, Peter, became his coach. Sebastian established three world marks in a span of 41 days in 1979 by setting records in the 800 meters, the 1500 meters, and the mile. He conquered a fourth distance when he broke the world record for the 1000 meters in 1980. At the 1980 Moscow Olympics, he captured a gold

medal in the 1500. In 1981, Coe lowered the world marks in the 800 and the 1000. He also broke the mile record twice in a 10-day span. He shaved more than a second off the mark with a time of 3 minutes, 47.33 seconds (3:47.33). At the 1984 Games in Los Angeles, Coe won the gold medal in the 1500, becoming the first man to capture the event in consecutive Olympics.

Most track-and-field competitors are driven by their desire to set records. But the only records that Sebastian Coe seemed to seek were the discs that he liked to spin on his stereo. The 22-year-old Englishman was becoming a star on the track circuit, yet he seemed content to enjoy his music, his college studies, and the finer things in life. When he competed, he seemed to be running just for fun.

On July 5, 1979, Sebastian Coe began one of the most amazing record-breaking stretches in track history. That day, he broke the world mark for the 800-meter run in Oslo, Norway. Twelve days later, he broke the record for the mile, again in Oslo. And on August 15—

41 days after his first record—he smashed the world mark in the 1500-meter run. The last record was set in Zurich, Switzerland.

After Coe had run his record mile, he remarked, "I honestly did not know what the world record was, except that it was just under 3 minutes, 50 seconds." Following his third world mark, the new track hero said, "It was the only occasion when I've gone consciously for a record."

Many track fans thought Coe's attitude was strange, but they did not know Sebastian Newbold Coe. He was born in London on September 29, 1956, and was raised by his parents, Peter and Angela Coe.

Growing up in Sheffield, England, he learned from his parents that athletics were only a part of life. He and the other three Coe children were taught to work hard in school and to appreciate the arts. The entire family enjoyed the theater and music.

"Seb," as he was called, was the only athlete in the family. He began running cross-country in his early teens. At 15, he became a promising 800-meter competitor, when he broke the two-minute mark for the first time. A year later, he was the English schoolboy 3000-meter champion. After that accomplishment, he ran primarily in half-mile and mile events.

Coe soon became a very serious runner. His father, who had no experience training other runners, became his coach. Peter Coe recalled: "When he was in age-group racing, he was a year younger than the rest. I told him to go along at the pace he knew he could hold. And he said: 'What will that get me?' I told him maybe a sixth place. He said: 'That's not for me, I'm running with the leaders.'"

Unlike many great runners, Seb refused to toil in extra-long training sessions. "I've never run longer than six miles in training," he would later tell a reporter, "and that was six miles too long."

Instead, Coe trained more like a sprinter, running as fast as he could for as far as he could. He called it speed endurance training. Experts had long felt that speed training alone was detrimental to a middle-distance runner, but Coe would soon prove them wrong.

Seb ran his first mile of less than four minutes when he was 19. He was making greater progress, however, in the 800 meters. At 20, he ran the distance in 1 minute, 45 seconds (1:45.0). By the next year, he was ranked third in the world.

Coe set his first world record in the 800 on July 5, 1979. His time was an astounding 1:42.4, a whole second under the record. The world mark had not come down a full second in the previous 15 years.

A slim 5 feet, 9 inches, and 129 pounds, Coe did not look like

Coe, Sebastian

an athlete who could battle the world's finest milers. But on July 17, he faced a dozen of the best. The field included John Walker of New Zealand, who held the outdoor record, and Eamonn Coghlan of Ireland, the indoor record-holder.

Coe approached the race with

Coe (Number 254) struggles to catch fellow countryman and rival Steve Ovett (Number 279) during the 800-meter run at the 1980 Olympics. Although Ovett won the race, Sebastian defeated him later in the 1500.

confidence. Against so many good runners, his strategy was not to have much strategy at all. "I run unconsciously, as if I am on an automatic pilot," he liked to say.

In the race, Seb stayed with the front runners, clocking 1:54.5 for the first half. He was in third place, but running faster than Walker had run when he set the record. He took the lead at the three-quarters mark, and then pulled away. His time was 3:49. Nine men finished the race in 3:54.5 or better, making it the fastest mile ever.

Great Britain's Sebastian Coe raises his arms in jubilation after setting a world record in the 800 meters at Oslo, Norway.

Less than a month later, Coe broke the five-year-old 1500 record

Coe crosses the finish line to win the 1500 at the 1984 Olympic Games in Los Angeles.

Coe shows a rare display of emotion after winning the 1500-meter race at the 1980 Olympics in Moscow.

with a time of 3:32.1. After setting his third world record in 41 days, Sebastian Coe became an international celebrity.

In July of 1980, Coe gained and lost a world record in Oslo, Norway. After establishing a 1000-meter mark of 2:13.4, he watched Steve Ovett clip his mile record by .2 of a second.

Later, Coe was asked how he felt he would do in the 1980 Olympic Games in Moscow. He replied, "The Games are littered with people who had one good day and were never heard of or seen again." He added that his studies in eco-

nomics and sociology were just as important to him. Despite his casual attitude, Coe won the 1500-meter event and placed second in the 800-meter race at the 1980 Olympics in Moscow.

A year later, Sebastian set the world marks in the 800 meters and the 1000 meters. He also broke the mile record twice within a 10-day span. In his second record-shattering mile run, he shaved more than a second off his world mark with a time of 3:47.33.

Injuries slowed the great distance runner over the next couple of years. By the arrival of the 1984 Olympics in Los Angeles, Coe was not considered a serious threat in the 1500. He was, however, a favorite to win the 800.

In the Games, he captured a silver medal in the 800 meters, finishing second to Joaquim Cruz of Brazil. Coe shocked the running world by taking the gold medal in the 1500 five days later. Competing in a strong field that included fellow countrymen Steve Ovett and Steve Cram, Sebastian smashed the Olympic mark with a clocking of 3:32.53. He had become the first man in history to win consecutive gold medals in the 1500-meter event.

In 1986, Coe was ranked the best distance runner at 800 meters and 1000 meters. By the time he retired in 1990, he had set 12 world records (eight outdoors and four indoors). In 1992, Coe was elected to the British Parliament.

⍢ Comaneci, Nadia

NAHD-YUH KOH-MUH-*NETCH* (1961-   ), gymnast, was born in Gheorghe Gheorghiu-Dej (Onesti), Rumania. She began her career at six when a talent-hunting coach discovered her at school. Less than two years later, Nadia competed in Rumania's junior national championship and finished in 13th place. She won the event the following year. In 1975, Nadia captured the European championship, her first senior international competition. At the 1976 Olympic Games in Montreal, Nadia Comaneci dazzled the sports world by displaying her perfection in gymnastics. She received seven perfect scores of 10.00. Nadia won gold

medals for her performances in the balance beam, the uneven parallel bars, and the all-around competitions. She also captured a silver medal in the team event and a bronze medal in the floor exercises. She was only 14 at the time. At the 1980 Moscow Olympics, Nadia won gold medals in the balance beam event and the floor exercises.

There is a popular saying that goes "Nobody's perfect." And it is easy to apply it to sports.

But then came the 1976 Olympic Games at Montreal, Quebec, Canada. There, a wisp of a girl from a small factory town in the Rumanian mountains displayed a show of perfection that would be difficult—if not impossible—to match. Her name was Nadia Comaneci, and she weighed all of 86 pounds.

Most sports fans, other than gymnastics experts, knew little about Comaneci when she was preparing for Montreal. Many were still recalling the exciting feats of Olga Korbut. As a teenager from the U.S.S.R., Olga got people interested in gymnastics with her performance at the 1972 Games. But in the 1976 Olympics, Nadia Comaneci stole the show.

Nadia became the star of that show when she captured a perfect 10.00 on the uneven parallel bars—a score no previous Olympian had received in any gymnastic event. But that was just the be-

ginning for Nadia. She registered two more perfect scores in the team competition the following night and seven in all during the competition at the Montreal Forum.

Gymnastics experts found it "astounding." Her number of perfect scores almost overshadowed her medal winnings. And her medal winnings included three golds, a silver, and a bronze.

Nadia had little to say later, except that she knew she would

Nadia performs gracefully on the balance beam.

Comaneci, Nadia

win. The man who had coached her, Bela Karolyi, knew she was a winner the first time he saw her.

Nadia was then at a kindergarten in the town of Gheorghe Gheorghiu-Dej (Onesti), Rumania, where she was born on November 12, 1961. Karolyi was on a talent search, looking for athletic youngsters he could begin to train at an early age. He noticed Nadia when he saw her and a friend playing alone in the school courtyard.

"They were running and jumping and pretending to be gymnasts," Karolyi recalled. "Then the bell rang, and they ran into the building and I lost them. I went into all the classes looking for them. I went again and still couldn't find them.

"A third time I went and asked, 'Who likes gymnastics?' In one of the classrooms, two girls sprang up. One is now a very promising ballerina. The other is Nadia."

Karolyi put Nadia and her friend through a series of tests to judge their skills. The tests included a sprint of 15 meters (about 16½ yards), a walk on a balance beam,

Nadia Comaneci, the 14-year-old from Rumania, won five medals at the 1976 Olympic Games in Montreal. She captured golds in the all-around, the balance beam, and the uneven parallel bars; a silver in the team competition; and a bronze in the floor exercise.

and a long jump. Nadia, the six-year-old daughter of a factory worker, did amazingly well.

She began training seriously in gymnastics at the boarding school she attended in her home town. In little more than a year, she was competing in her country's junior championship. Nadia was the youngest competitor, but she still finished 13th. Karolyi found her performance good—and a bad omen, because of the number 13.

"That was unlucky," he said. "I bought her an Eskimo doll for good luck and told her she must never rank 13th again."

She obeyed. The next year, she won the event.

Nadia continued to win in her own country and in international competition. In 1975, she captured the European championship, seizing the title from the great Soviet gymnast Ludmila Tourischeva. Nadia's collection of medals and dolls began to grow.

By 1976, she had collected 200 dolls that she kept stacked neatly on her bedroom shelves. Nadia Comaneci had become the best female gymnast in the world, though fans still talked about Olga Korbut. Yet when the 14-year-old

The first gymnast in history to score a perfect 10, Nadia Comaneci received three of them in the balance-beam competition.

Comaneci, Nadia

Rumanian scored her first perfect 10, the crowds turned to her.

"She is like a little wind-up doll," one spectator said of the expressionless Comaneci.

Her perfect score on the uneven parallel bars was not her first one. Nadia had done that many times before. But that she did it in Olympic competition made it all the more important.

A minor controversy arose among some of the Russian judges who complained of the high scores

In her best event—the uneven parallel bars—Nadia scored perfect 10's to capture the gold medal at the 1976 Olympics.

she was given. Nadia reacted to the protest by saying, "I knew it [the performance on the bars] was flawless. I have done it 15 times before."

When Nadia outdid Olga Korbut with another perfect score on Olga's specialty, the balance beam, there was little to protest. Nadia had to be at her best, because Olga scored 9.90. That same evening, Nadia repeated a perfect

score of 10 on the parallel bars.

The *New York Times* reported: "Tonight's program may have been the most spectacular display of women's gymnastics ever."

Everyone was scoring high, but Nadia was outscoring everyone —with perfection. And she was just beginning.

"I'd like to do better than before," she said of the next competition set for two days later. "I'd like to better myself. But I was really glad and I felt very good tonight.

The grace and beauty of Nadia Comaneci, on her way to another perfect score of 10.

I think I've done well."

The 36 gymnasts who continued in the competition, the judges, and the 18,000 fans were all in awe as Nadia sparkled once more. Some of the enthusiastic spectators had paid scalpers up to $200 for $16 seats. Nadia received two more perfect scores in the all-around competition—one each on the beam and parallel bars. She was also close to perfection on the horse vault, with a 9.85 score. And she was at her best ever in the floor exercise, where she scored 9.90.

Her success that night gave her the gold medal for the individual all-around title, rating her as the best gymnast in the world. By then, even the Russians were beginning to appreciate her. As Nadia approached the victory stand to collect one of her gold medals, Ludmila Tourischeva—for years the finest all-around gymnast—followed her up the steps and gave her a victory kiss.

Officials were appreciating her, too. "I think she's the best gymnast the world has ever known," said Frank Bare, director of the U.S. Gymnastics Federation. "Technique-wise, form-wise, and execution-wise, she takes the basic points

Nadia executes a backward flip on the balance beam.

Comaneci, Nadia

of a routine and does it higher and better than anyone. She's as steady as can be."

On the final night of the individual-apparatus competition, Nadia scored two more perfect 10s.

For the 1976 Olympics, Nadia won gold medals in the uneven parallel bars, the balance beam, and all-around competition. She won a silver in the team event, with Rumania placing second to the Russians. She also won a bronze in the floor exercises. In her floor routines, Nadia performed to the American music "Yes, Sir, That's My Baby" and "The Young and the Restless" ("Nadia's Theme"). In her other event, the vault, she just missed a medal by placing fourth.

Nadia Comaneci was the star of the Olympics. Although she was still a ninth-grader, gymnastics had become a very serious business for her.

"It used to be fun," she told a reporter. "It was like playing a game. Now it is work. I must practice three to four hours a day. I enjoy the sport, but I must work very hard."

Coach Bela Karolyi listed the reasons why his star gymnast was so good: "The physical qualities—strength, speed, agility. The intellectual qualities—intelligence and the power to concentrate. And Nadia has courage."

Nadia earned her third straight European championship in 1979.

In an Associated Press poll, Comaneci was selected the Female Athlete of the Year for 1976.

By 1979, Nadia had grown to 5 feet, 3½ inches, and 106 pounds. The next year, at the Moscow Olympics, Nadia won the balance beam event and tied for first in the floor exercises.

The world-renowned gymnast accomplished her most courageous feat in 1989. She defected from her native country, Rumania, to North America.

In her new home, Nadia took part in gymnastics exhibitions. She performed with former U.S. Olympic champion Bart Conner.

A high point at the 1976 Olympics was Nadia's floor exercise.

⊖Connolly, Maureen

(1934-1969), tennis player, was born in San Diego, California. She began playing tennis at 10 and shortly after came under the guidance of the famed tennis coach Eleanor "Teach" Tennant. Maureen Connolly took part in many tournaments from 1944 to 1950, and in 1948 she won her first major title, the U.S. national junior championship. Becoming the youngest modern player to do so, she won the U.S. women's singles championship at 16. In 1952, 1953, and 1954, she ranked as the greatest woman tennis player in the world. She was named the Associated Press Woman Athlete of the Year in those years. In her best year, 1953, "Little Mo," as she was often referred to, won the Grand Slam of tennis—the U.S. crown at Forest Hills, the All-England title at Wimbledon, the French Open championship, and the Australian Open championship. By doing so, she became the first woman to capture all four titles

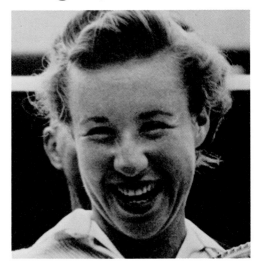

in one year. It looked as if she was going to repeat her feat in 1954. But a serious horseback riding accident permanently damaged her leg and ended her career at 19. She was later married to Norman Brinker, a former Olympic equestrain. Until her death in 1969, Maureen Connolly devoted herself to teaching tennis to youngsters.

When Maureen Connolly was only 18, she reached a high point in tennis that no woman player had ever reached before. She won the Grand Slam—taking the American, Australian, French, and British championships. It put her in a class with the game's greatest players. The next year, she might have repeated her great performance, but a terrible accident left her crippled.

Maureen was able to stand and hit the ball, but she was never able to play again.

Maureen Connolly was born in San Diego, California, on September 17, 1934. Her father was a chief petty officer in the Navy; her mother was a gifted organist.

Her father died when Maureen was two years old, and she was

raised by her mother and her great aunt. As a child, Maureen was a talented rider, entering horse shows and winning prizes.

When she was 10 years old, the family moved to a house near the Balboa city tennis courts, where Maureen often went to watch the players. While watching a hard, serious match between two strong

Maureen returns a shot to Doris Hart in the women's singles finals in the Wimbledon Tennis Championships in 1953. That year she completed a Grand Slam by winning the U.S., British, French, and Australian titles.

and it proved to be good.

Maureen entered her first tournament while still only 10 years old. She reached the final match of the 13-and-under singles and lost to Ann Bissell. Being runner-up was a bitter let-down for Maureen, who had a fierce desire to be best. She practiced harder than before, to be ready for Ann Bissell in the next tournament.

She and Ann Bissell both reached the finals again. Maureen had much less experience than the older girl, but she had tremendous ability and a strong will to win. This time, she beat Ann Bissell and won the tournament. The Balboa Club honored the young singles champion with a free membership.

Maureen Connolly entered more tournaments in Southern California. While she was practicing at Griffith Park in Los Angeles, her smooth, strong game was noticed by Mrs. Daisy Tree, a leading California tennis player. Mrs. Tree arranged for Eleanor "Teach" Tennant, a nationally famous tennis coach, to watch Maureen play. "Teach" Tennant had earlier coached Bobby Riggs and Alice Marble.

"Teach" saw in Maureen Connolly the makings of a player who could win in national and world tennis competition.

The teacher was as dedicated to tennis as her new student. She understood Maureen's great spirit. As the future star developed, her coach managed a careful balance of discipline, hard work, and encouragement.

Probably no woman ever played with greater self-discipline than Maureen Connolly, and she had a natural knack for tennis tac-

men players, she made up her mind that tennis was a game she would master. Tennis pro Wilbur Folsom, who taught tennis at the city courts, saw her watching his classes and invited her to join them. Folsom soon saw that she had a burning ambition to master the game. He gently and skillfully guided her first steps toward greatness.

Folsom told his young student, a left-handed hitter, that she would be a better tennis player as a right-hander. She followed his advice,

Connolly, Maureen

tics. Almost every shot she made was part of a plan.

The 5-foot, 5-inch, 130-pound wonder, nicknamed "Little Mo," practiced four and five hours a day. Her daring shots, placed close to the line, were very hard to return.

For an hour or more before the beginning of a match, Maureen could think about nothing else and would talk to no one. She played a hard-driving game, never giving an opponent an easy point. After a match, she needed as much as half an hour to unwind before talking to friends or reporters.

But off the court, Maureen was a bubbling, happy, and friendly girl who loved baseball, dancing, and music of all kinds. She said, "You have to be able to relax between matches and between tournaments."

From 1944 to 1950, Maureen Connolly played in more and more important tournaments. "Teach" Tennant chose the ones that would help her pupil strengthen her game. Slowly, she built her up to the supreme challenge of world championship tennis.

In 1948, when Maureen was 14, she won her first major title, the United States national junior championship.

In 1951, when she was 16, Maureen entered the U.S. National women's singles tournament at Forest Hills, New York. Throughout the tournament she played a cool, steady game that reminded watchers of Helen Wills Moody. In the final match she took the first set from Shirley Fry, 6-3, by powerful hitting that brought gasps from the crowd. Maureen Connolly lost the second set, then won the match by taking the third set, 6-4. The new 16-year-old national champion screamed, then wept with joy and relief.

Maureen Connolly was a year younger than Helen Wills had been when she won the title in 1923.

As a member of the Wightman Cup team in 1951, 1952, and 1953, Maureen won every match she played. In 1951, she was ranked second in world tennis after Doris Hart. In 1952, 1953, and 1954, she was ranked first.

In 1952, Maureen Connolly won the U.S. championship at Forest Hills again and won the All-England title at Wimbledon. The Associated Press named her Woman Athlete of the Year, as they did again in 1953 and 1954.

Her biggest year was 1953. She beat Doris Hart for the U.S. crown at Forest Hills and won the All-England title at Wimbledon, the French Open championship, and the Australian Open championship. Maureen Connolly was the first woman to win all four matches in one year. Her Grand Slam was not repeated until 17 years later, when Margaret Smith Court won all four in 1970.

In 1954, Maureen looked like a good bet to repeat the Grand Slam. She won at Wimbledon and she won the French Open. She also won in the French Open doubles and the French Open mixed doubles. But she could not compete at Forest Hills or in the Australian Open, because of a bad accident while riding horseback.

In July 1954, the 19-year-old superstar went riding with two friends. She rode a thoroughbred horse that had been given to her by her neighbors in San Diego. Maureen loved riding almost as much as she loved tennis. As they rode along a path beside a highway, the noise from an approaching truck frightened her horse. The horse bolted into the side of the truck, which struck the tennis star's leg, knocking her off the horse and into a ditch.

She was sure she would never be able to continue her tennis career. To help her leg heal, she studied dance and had many hours of physical therapy. But the main artery in her leg was permanently injured, and muscles and tendons were deeply cut. There was no

more chance of playing competition tennis.

Later that year she married Norman Brinker, a former member of the U.S. Olympic equestrian team.

In February 1955, Maureen Connolly announced her retirement from tennis. Marrying Norman Brinker, she said, "I've had a full life with lots of travel and I've met lots of wonderful people. Now I'm going to be a little housewife. It's a new career and I'm awfully happy with it." They had two children.

She became active in the

The Duchess of Kent (right) presents the Wimbledon Trophy to Maureen Connolly in 1954 when she won her third straight Wimbledon championship.

Maureen Connolly Brinker Foundation in Texas, for helping junior players. Until her death in 1969, she devoted herself to teaching the game to youngsters. She said, "My strokes are as good as ever. But if the ball is out of reach I have to let it go."

In 1968, Maureen Connolly was elected to the International Tennis Hall of Fame in Newport, Rhode Island. She died of cancer on June 21, 1969.

⊖ Connors, Jimmy (1952-   ),

tennis player, was born in East St. Louis, Illinois. He was introduced to tennis at an early age by his mother, a tennis pro, and his grandmother, a former tournament player. He won the first tournament he ever entered—the Southern Illinois for boys under 10. When he was 16, his mother sent him to California to train under former tennis great Pancho Segura. After high school, Connors attended the University of California at Los Angeles (UCLA). There, he won the National Collegiate Athletic Association (NCAA) singles title as a freshman. Connors turned pro in 1972. Soon, he was ranked among the world's best players. He captured the Australian, Wimbledon, and U.S. Open championships in 1974, becoming the top player

in the world. In 1976, Connors won 12 tournaments, including the U.S. Open. Among his later victories were the World Championship Tennis (WCT) title in 1977 and 1980, Wimbledon in 1982, and the U.S. Open in 1978, 1982, and 1983. Ranked among the world's top 10 players for 16 years, Jimmy Connors held the Open era record for singles titles with 109.

In the 1970's, tennis rose to become one of the most popular sports in the world. Among the many stars who quickly became internationally famous, none gained more recognition than Jimmy Connors, the brash young man from Illinois.

In 1976, Connors, who was just 25 years old, made $303,335 on the tennis circuit and about $600,000 overall for his matches. His name was known to all sports fans in the U.S. and abroad.

Connors was lucky that tennis became so popular in the 1970's. But it was not luck that brought him so many victories. Some critics of the sport thought that he was as good as any player who ever lived. Others felt that he could become the greatest.

James Scott Connors grew up playing tennis. He was born on September 2, 1952, in East St. Louis, Illinois. His mother, Gloria Thompson Connors, was a teaching professional. His grandmother, who also influenced Jimmy's career, had been a tournament pro. As a youth, Jimmy spent endless hours on the court that they had set up for practice in the backyard.

"He took up the game as if it were part of him," his mother said.

Jimmy Connors was quick to defend his mother against charges of pressuring him into the game. "People have criticized my mom for trying to make me what she wasn't," he once told a reporter. "But the peons don't realize this is what I've always wanted to be. Tennis is my choice, my life."

Jimmy began playing in tournaments and won the very first one he participated in—the Southern Illinois tournament for boys under 10. His whole life revolved around the game. Connors has said that he had little time for friends at school. Jimmy hardly knew his fellow students because he would rush out after classes to be at courtside.

His mother and grandmother helped him with his game. They would take him to tournaments, drive him to and from practice after school, and practice with him.

At 16, when he was doing well locally but not nationally, a decision was made to send Jimmy to Beverly Hills, California. There, he could train under tennis great Pancho Segura. Connors attended a private high school (Rexford) in Beverly Hills so that his schedule could revolve around tennis.

After graduation, he enrolled at the University of California at Los Angeles (UCLA). Connors was ready for national competition. As a freshman, Jimmy startled the tennis world by winning the National Collegiate Athletic Asso-

Connors, Jimmy

ciation (NCAA) singles title.

Soon, Jimmy could defeat such greats as Roy Emerson, Stan Smith, and Clark Graebner. He decided to turn professional in January of 1972. Connors enlisted tour promoter Bill Riordan as his manager. Later, in 1975, he severed relations with Riordan.

As a professional, Connors won his first two tournaments. He made it to the quarter-finals at Wimbledon (England) and wound up capturing more victories for the year than any American pro. He had 75 in all and collected $90,000 for his efforts.

The following year, Connors became the "tiger on the court" that his mother had taught him to be. He became the youngest winner of the U.S. Pro Championship and held his own in most tournaments. Jimmy became a specialist in singles play. He did not like doubles.

"No one's ever given me anything on the court," he said. "It's just you and me. When I win, I don't have to congratulate anyone. When I lose, I don't have to blame anyone."

In 1974, Jimmy Connors was the outstanding player in the world, winning the Australian

Connors is noted for his powerful ground strokes.

Open, the Wimbledon title, and the U.S. Open championship. Banned from competing in the French Open because he played for the Baltimore Banners in the newly formed World Team Tennis (WTT) league, Connors lost his chance to win tennis' Grand Slam.

In the All-England tournament at Wimbledon, Connors won the men's singles title by smashing Ken Rosewall in the finals (6-1, 6-1, 6-4). At the time, he was engaged to Chris Evert, one of the best women players in the world. Chris won the women's singles title that year. The tremendous publicity that accompanied their double win eventually helped to end their wedding plans.

After capturing the grass-court championship at Wimbledon, Connors returned home. There, he won the U.S. Clay Court title. Then came the U.S. Open in Forest Hills, New York. Once again, Connors easily defeated Rosewall (6-1, 6-0, 6-1)—the most lopsided men's finals in the 93 years of Forest Hills Competition.

Jimmy Connors money winnings grew to $285,490 in 1974. He won 14 of 20 tournaments.

Though his 1975 season was not quite as successful and dramatic

Jimmy does a little jig after winning a point.

Connors, Jimmy

In 1974, Jimmy Connors and Chris Evert were the Wimbledon singles champions. Shown with their trophies, the two were engaged to be married at the time.

as the year before, he had earned the respect of many of his peers on the court.

"You have to know how to serve to beat Connors," said Australian John Newcombe, who beat him in the 1975 finals of the Australian Open. "Serving to Connors is like pitching to Hank Aaron. If you don't mix it up, he'll hit it out of the ballpark."

But not everyone respected Connors. For his antics on the court, he got a "bad boy" image. Many of his opponents criticized him. They called him a smart aleck, a prima donna, a poor sport, and immature.

"I'm cocky and confident," Connors said in his own defense. "And maybe I'm too bullheaded sometimes. But I think I have *some* humility."

Even his worst enemies respected Connors' tennis skills. His serves were not overpowering. But his strong ground strokes, slashing returns, two-handed backhands, running stamina, and savage play kept his opponents under constant pressure. One thing Connors especially prided himself on was his return of serves.

Connors confined his off-court interests to personal things. He played backgammon games with close friends and enjoyed singing. He had wanted to be a singer when he attended UCLA.

In 1976, his game was better than *ever*. He began winning one important tournament after another—the U.S. Pro Indoor, the American Airlines Games, the Alan King Classic, the U.S. Clay Court. He also captured his third challenge match, beating Manuel Orantes. In previous years, he had defeated Rod Laver and John Newcombe in challenge matches.

By August, Connors was ready for the big one—the U.S. Open at Forest Hills, New York. There, he faced Swedish star Björn Borg, who had won 19 straight matches

Watching the ball all the way to the racket, Connors strokes a fine two-handed backhand.

Connors, Jimmy

At age 39, veteran Jimmy Connors dazzled crowds at the 1991 U.S. Open. Connors advanced all the way to the semifinals.

Connors displays his trophy at the 1974 U.S. Open in Forest Hills, New York. In the finals, he defeated Ken Rosewall in straight sets.

going into the final. The crowd at the West Side Tennis Club roared with excitement during the final match.

They were the two best players of the year—young men from different sides of the world who, according to *Sports Illustrated* magazine, "had divided all the spoils in sight" before coming together near the end of one of tennis' greatest seasons.

In over three hours of heated competition—which some critics called the greatest tennis ever played—Connors won (6-4, 3-6, 7-6, 6-4). Connors, who had now defeated Borg six out of seven times in head-to-head competition, was elated.

"It was the best tennis I ever played," he said. "I feel I've dominated the game this year. But Björn had WCT [World Championship Tennis] and Wimbledon so I wanted him here."

The statistics bore out Connors dominance of the game in 1976. He won 91 per cent of his matches. His earnings on the tour were a record $303,335, and about $600,000 overall.

Later, Connors' major triumphs included the 1977 and 1980 WCT titles, the 1978 U.S. Open and Grand Prix Masters, and the 1979 U.S. Clay Court title.

By the early 1980's, many experts considered Connors a "has been." He silenced those critics by winning the Wimbledon championship in 1982 and two more U.S. Open titles in 1982 and 1983.

In 1990, Connors started doing analysis of televised tennis matches. He also had wrist surgery. Then, in 1991, he stunned the tennis world by reaching the semifinals at the U.S. Open.

For over 20 years, Jimmy Connors was a force on the court.

⊖ Court, Margaret (1942-),

tennis player, was born Margaret Smith in Albury, New South Wales, Australia. She started playing tennis with her brothers at an area court and shortly after began taking tennis lessons with the local pro. By the time Margaret was 15, she had won 60 trophies. Her parents then sent her to Melbourne, where she was coached by Frank Sedgman, the Wimbledon and Davis Cup champion. Margaret became the youngest woman in history to win the Australian Senior International Championship at 17. She won the Australian title again in 1961. From 1962 through 1966, she won almost every tennis title and championship. Following a temporary retirement at the end of 1966, Margaret Court returned to competitive tennis in 1968.

She became the first woman since Maureen Connolly to win the Grand Slam (the U.S. Open, the All-England title at Wimbledon, the French Open, and the Australian Open) in 1970. In all types of play, Margaret Court won over 60 championship titles in Grand Slam tournaments, more than any other player in history. Of those, a record 24 were singles crowns.

Margaret Smith Court was always a shy and nervous player. Yet she won more top tennis titles — Australian, French, British, and American — than any other player in tennis history. In 1970, she became the first woman since Maureen Connolly to win the Grand Slam — all of the Big Four titles in one year.

Margaret Smith was born in Albury, New South Wales, Australia, on July 16, 1942. She was the youngest of four children. Her father was a foreman in the dairy business.

Margaret first played tennis when a neighbor gave her an old racket. She and her brothers often sneaked onto the public tennis courts near their home. There was one court where they could play without being seen, if one player always played close to the net. This was Margaret's position. "That must have been where I learned to volley," she said later. "The boys banged shots at me as hard as they could, and I just had to reach them if we wanted to go on playing."

The tennis pro got tired of chasing her off the courts and began giving her lessons. Later, he began arranging tennis matches for her.

Margaret was a natural tennis player. By the time she was 15, she had won 60 trophies. Her

Racing over at the last second, Margaret returns a shot at the All-England Lawn Tennis Championships at Wimbledon.

Court, Margaret

British royalty was on hand in 1970 as Princess Margaret presented Margaret Court a silver plate for her victory in the women's singles finals of the All-England Lawn Tennis Championships at Wimbledon.

parents then sent her to Melbourne to be coached by Frank Sedgman, a Wimbledon and Davis Cup champion of the 1950's.

At 17, she became the youngest woman ever to win the Australian Senior International Championship. But Sedgman told her to wait a year before playing in tournaments outside Australia. Margaret worked hard in 1960 to improve her game.

In 1961, she won the Aus-

tralian title again, then joined the Australian tennis team for its world tour. She was 19 and in top form, but she was not yet ready for the pressure of playing in world tennis matches against more experienced players.

The next year, she made it to the final match at Wimbledon, but all the publicity she got seemed to take away her confidence. She lost to 18-year-old Billie Jean Moffitt (now Billie Jean King). After the match, the champion said, "I feel sorry for Margaret. She is a great player, but there was too much pressure on her." The disappointed Margaret Smith said, "I'll be back next year."

From 1962 through 1966, Margaret Smith won nearly every title there was to win in tennis. Her confidence grew. But every game was still a trial for her. Finally, at the end of the 1966 season, she retired. Margaret said, "I've won everything, and I'm bored with tennis."

The tennis star went home to Australia and opened a dress shop. Then she met Barry Court, a well-to-do businessman, and they were married on October 28, 1967. Tennis was far from Margaret Court's thoughts until she began hitting a few balls for fun at a friend's house. Barry Court began talking about how he would like to see the world. "The next thing I knew, Margaret was back on tour," says her husband.

In 1968, Margaret Court won the U.S. National singles championship, the U.S. Open doubles championship (with Maria Bueno), and the South African singles championship.

In 1969, she won the Australian National championship and the U.S. Open championship.

One of Margaret Court's toughest and most exciting matches was against Billie Jean King in 1970 at Wimbledon. They played 46

Playing with a heavily taped left ankle, Margaret still defeated Rosemary Casals in the semifinals of the All-England Lawn Tennis Championships in 1970.

Court, Margaret

Margaret digs for a backhand return during the 1973 U.S. Open at Forest Hills, New York. She won the championship—marking her fifth U.S. Open title.

games in two and a half hours. Margaret finally won, 14-12, 11-9. She went on to win the French and Australian Opens. She had now won three of the Big Four in one season.

On September 13, 1970, she faced Rosemary Casals in the final match of the U.S. Open at Forest Hills, New York. She had a chance to be the first woman since Maureen Connolly to win the Grand Slam. Top-seeded in the tournament, Margaret Court was nervous. Her game suffered. She had 30 errors in the first two sets—more than in any of the preliminary rounds. In spite of her errors, she beat Rosemary Casals, 6-2, 2-6, 6-1. She had won the Grand Slam!

The following year, Margaret Court won the South African and the Irish Open titles, the London championship, and Rothman's British Hardcourt championship.

Margaret did not play during the 1972 season because she was pregnant. Her son, Daniel, was born in March 1972. Late in the season, she entered the Virginia Slims tournament tour. She was a consistent winner on the tour in 1973. That year, Margaret Court also won the singles and doubles

Two competitors eye the trophy given in the $100,000 Virginia Slims Tennis Tournament. At one time, Margaret Court (right) and Billie Jean King were considered the best women tennis players in the world.

In 1973, Bobby Riggs (top), the 55-year-old former Wimbledon champion, challenged Margaret to a "tennis battle of the sexes." In the one-match tournament, Riggs defeated Margaret, 6-2, 6-1, to win the $20,000 prize. Margaret Court took home $10,000.

titles of the Australian, French, and U.S. Opens, nearly capturing the Grand Slam. She was the top money-winner for the year.

After taking a maternity leave in 1974, Margaret Court returned the following year. She captured the doubles title with Virginia Wade at the U.S. Open and the mixed-doubles crown with Marty Riessen at the Wimbledon championships. In April 1975, she signed a one-year contract with the Hawaii Leis of World Team Tennis (WTT).

When 1977 came around, Margaret Court was still competing on the women's tour. Her height (5 feet, 9 inches) and long reach had always made it difficult for opponents to get shots past her. Though she was no longer the dominant figure in women's tennis that she once had been, she still was quick and could cover the court with a few strides.

Counting singles, doubles, and mixed doubles, Margaret Court won over 60 championship titles in the tournaments that comprise the Grand Slam—more than any other player in history. Of those, a record 24 were singles crowns.

"Whenever you talk of great women tennis players," said Marty Riessen, who held many mixed-doubles titles with Margaret Court, "you have to start with Margaret. She should go down as the finest woman player of all time."

✦Cousy, Bob *KOO-ZEE* (1928-),

basketball player, was born in New York City. Playing basketball constantly as a youth, Bob was at first considered too small for the sport. At Andrew Jackson High School in Queens, he made the all-city team in his senior year. Cousy was a 1950 All-America selection at the College of the Holy Cross in Worcester, Massachusetts. With the Boston Celtics of the National Basketball Association (NBA), Cousy became one of the best small guards to play the game, exhibiting sparkling ball-handling and play-making. He helped the Celtics capture six league championships and made the NBA All-Star first team for 10

straight seasons. In 1957, Bob Cousy was named the league's Most Valuable Player. When he retired, Cousy ranked first in career assists. He was voted to the Basketball Hall of Fame in 1970. Cousy coached at Boston College and then with the Cincinnati Royals (later the Kansas City-Omaha Kings). He became the first full-time commissioner of the American Soccer League in 1975.

Basketball's "case for the little man" was perhaps best made by Bob Cousy, the backcourt wizard of the Boston Celtics during the late 1950's and early 1960's.

While the Wilt Chamberlains and Bill Russells were threatening to turn the pro game into a sport dominated by the big man, it was Cousy—with his magical ball-handling, passing skill, and play-making—who proved the value of a quick-handed guard.

A native of New York City, Robert Cousy was born August 9, 1928. Although he was first inter-ested in baseball, Cousy became a basketball fanatic. It was all he cared about—he would eat, drink, and sleep the sport. When he reached Andrew Jackson High School in Queens, he became an all-city performer. In 1947, he entered the College of the Holy Cross in Worcester, Massachusetts. Until his graduation in 1950, Cousy was a member of the Holy Cross basketball team. He averaged 15.1 points per game and was named All-American in 1950.

In spite of his fine play in college, 6-foot, 1-inch Cousy did not receive much notice by the NBA teams. He was eventually chosen by the Tri-Cities Hawks and then traded to the Chicago Stags. The Stags folded soon afterward—and Cousy's name, along with the names of Andy Phillip and Max Zaslofsky, was put into a hat for a drawing by the New York, Philadel-phia, and Boston teams. Walter Brown, owner of the Celtics, later said he never made a more lucky draw than when he picked out the

Smallness is no hindrance to Cousy (Number 14) as he drives past the Minneapolis Lakers' Bob Leonard during a 1959 Celtics-Lakers battle.

Cousy, Bob

Slipping between two Los Angeles defenders, Cousy leads a Boston fast break during his final season with the Celtics in 1963.

name of Bob Cousy.

For the next 13 seasons, Bob Cousy sparked the play of the Boston Celtics. Six times he helped them to the NBA championship. He acted as the Celtics' leading playmaker for all of his 13 seasons on the team.

Best known for his almost magical ball-handling, Cousy was able to change his speed and direction instantly—while keeping firm control of the ball he was dribbling.

His noted "behind-the-back" dribble became a trademark that no other player was able to match. His play also inspired the "fast break" in basketball.

Besides his many other skills, Bob Cousy led the Celtics in scoring four straight seasons—1951-1955 —and set the NBA record for assists in one game, collecting 28 against the Minneapolis Lakers on February 27, 1959. By the end of his pro career, Cousy was first in total assists with 6955. He had a career

total of 16,960 points, an average of 18.4 per game. Bob Cousy's performance earned him the honor of being selected for the NBA All-Star first team 10 times. He received the NBA's Most-Valuable-Player award in 1957.

Basketball may never see another Cousy. Considered by many —pros and fans alike—as the flashiest player ever to hit the NBA, Bob Cousy was one of a kind. Some of his opponents have admitted that they were so taken with

Bob Cousy was not in the least predictable about his moves. During this 1958 playoff game, Cousy goes up to shoot, but then decides to flip a pass back to a surprised Bill Russell (Number 6).

A top college ballplayer at Holy Cross, Cousy drives in to score a lay-up against NYU in 1949.

Cousy makes a successful move past one of the NBA's superstars, Oscar Robertson.

Cousy's spectacular play that they were tempted just to stand there on the court and admire his tricky moves.

The great guard retired at the end of the 1962-1963 season. *New York Times* columnist Arthur Daley wrote, "It was a thrill to watch this artist make so blazing a departure and yet it brought with it jumbled emotions, an inescapable sadness. It was like watching Ted Williams hit his farewell home run, the sense of loss one experiences with the realization that we may never see his like again."

Retiring from active play, Bob Cousy became basketball coach at Boston College. From 1963 through 1969, his teams rolled up a record of 118 wins against 38 losses and took part in five post-season tournaments.

But there was one unhappy event that marred his years at Boston College. In October 1967, Bob Cousy was falsely accused of giving information on the point spread of his team's games to professional gamblers. A story about his "connection" with two gamblers was printed in *Life* magazine. Cousy called a news conference to deny the charges—and the National Collegiate Athletic Association (NCAA) and the public agreed that he was innocent. Cousy was cleared of any wrongdoing. "My conscience is clear," Cousy said, "but 21 years of my life have been affected by this, and it seems a high price to pay for something that isn't

Cousy, Bob

Choked with emotion, Cousy pauses while speaking to the 15,000 fans who came to honor him on "Bob Cousy Night." The event preceded his last regular-season game with the Celtics at Boston Garden in 1963.

backed by any real evidence." The matter was dropped and, for the most part, forgotten.

Coaching at the college level demands a great deal of recruiting, since a new crop of freshmen players must be found each year. Bob Cousy did not enjoy that side of coaching, and so, in 1969, he signed a pro contract to coach the Cincinnati Royals. In his first season, he also played in seven games.

Cousy was called on to begin the difficult task of helping the Royals (a team that later became the Kansas City-Omaha Kings) climb from the lower ranks of the NBA. In his attempt to start a rebuilding program, Cousy was harshly criticized for trading away star players Jerry Lucas and Oscar Robertson. He enlisted the aid of a small, quick guard, Nate Archibald, whose ball-handling skills reminded fans of Cousy's own heydey. Unable to make the team a winner, Cousy retired from coaching in 1973.

The name Bob Cousy will long be remembered in basketball. In 1970, the great play-making guard was enshrined in the Basketball Hall of Fame.

Bob Cousy returned to professional sports in 1975. He became the first full-time commissioner of the American Soccer League.

Celtic coach Red Auerbach gives Bob Cousy a hug. Cousy finished his 13-year pro basketball career with Boston by leading the club to a fifth straight NBA title in 1963.

🏈 Csonka, Larry ZONK-UH (1946-   ),

football player, was born in Stow, Ohio. In high school, he was active in football, wrestling, and track. Later, he attended Syracuse University. He began playing linebacker on the football squad and moved to fullback in his sophomore year. Csonka went on to break the rushing records of such former Syracuse stars as Jim Brown, Ernie Davis, and Floyd Little. He became the first player in college history to be selected as the outstanding player in both the College All-Star and the Coaches' All-American games. Csonka, picked by the Miami Dolphins, was the first running back chosen in the American Football League (AFL) player draft of 1968. Known for his brute strength and hard hitting, he gained over 1000 yards rushing each season from 1971 through 1973. Csonka

helped lead the Dolphins to Super Bowl victories in 1973 and 1974. He was named the Most Valuable Player in the Super Bowl following the 1973 season. He played the 1975 season in the World Football League (WFL) and ended his career in the National Football League (NFL) with the New York Giants and Miami. Csonka was elected to the Pro Football Hall of Fame in 1987.

The Miami Dolphins compiled a 17-0 record during the 1972-1973 season—the first undefeated season in the National Football League (NFL) since 1942 (when the Chicago Bears were 11-0) and the best record in pro football history. One reason for the Dolphins' outstanding showing was the performance of running back Larry Csonka.

In that year, Csonka, a throw-back to the old days with his hard-driving running style, ranked as the number-two ball-carrier in the American Football Conference (AFC). He rushed for 1117 yards in 213 carries—an average of 5.2 yards per carry.

In 1971, Csonka became the first Dolphin ever to gain over 1000 yards (1051), for a league-leading average of 5.4 yards per carry. In both 1971 and 1972, Larry Csonka made every All-NFL team.

At Syracuse University, Csonka was a unanimous choice for the All-America team. He broke the rushing records of such earlier Syracuse greats as Jim Brown, Ernie Davis, Jim Nance, and Floyd Little. In 937 carries, Csonka gained 2934 career yards for a 4.9 average, always running against defenses built to stop him.

Csonka was the only player in history to be chosen the outstanding player in both the Coaches' All-

Csonka, Larry

American Game and the College All-Star Game. He was also the first offensive back picked in the pro draft of 1968, when he was selected by the Dolphins.

In NFL play, Csonka always used his own special way to get more yardage. Just before he was tackled, he dropped his head and rammed it into the tackler. Usually, it got him extra yardage, since he hit with explosive power.

His battering style was successful but left its effect on him. In 1970, he had a severe head injury, and from that time he wore a specially padded helmet.

Yet injuries seldom slowed Csonka. His nose was broken time after time. As a rookie, he suffered three violent blows to the skull. It was feared that he was through as a player when doctors found a crack at the base of his skull.

Besides these injuries, Csonka also had a cracked eardrum, broken blood vessels over his eye, and had surgery to remove bone chips from his elbow. In 1973, because of a back injury in the Super Bowl game, he was unable to play in the Pro Bowl. And in the years that followed, Csonka was hobbled by injuries that forced him to miss games. Yet he still

As a Syracuse University fullback, Csonka carries for a four-yard gain against UCLA in a 1966 contest.

Csonka (right) with Miami backfield mate Jim Kiick. Known as "Butch Cassidy and the Sundance Kid," they formed a fine running tandem in the Dolphins' title years.

Against the Pittsburgh Steelers, Larry goes for a long gain.

Csonka, Larry

Csonka breaks into the open and heads for a touchdown.

kept playing professional ball.

For all the violence of his play, Csonka rarely fumbled. "Playing for Ben Schwartzwalder at Syracuse, I learned not to fumble," Csonka later recalled. "They play a running game and fumbling is inexcusable. If you do, you'd better have a broken finger as an excuse."

At Miami, Csonka teamed up first with Jim Kiick. Nicknamed "Butch Cassidy and the Sundance Kid," they were one of the finest backfield combinations in football. They blocked for each other as few running backs have ever done.

After Miami lost to Oakland in the 1970 AFC playoffs, the determined Csonka and Kiick swore they would make it to the Super

After a year in the World Football League, Csonka returned to the NFL and played with the New York Giants. Here, he busts up the middle against the Redskins.

Bowl the next season.

Their vows proved true. In 1971, the Dolphins dropped only three games. Then they beat Kansas City and Baltimore in the conference playoffs, only to lose to Dallas in the Super Bowl.

The next year, the Dolphins surged through their entire season unbeaten. Csonka was teamed with lightning-quick Mercury Morris in the backfield. Csonka had the size to power up the middle and Morris had the speed to sweep outside. In 1972, they became the first running backs from the same team to each gain 1000 yards or more in a season. The Dolphins capped the year with a 14-7 victory against the Washington Redskins in the 1973 Super

Bowl. Csonka picked up 112 yards in the game, averaging 7.5 yards per carry. Once again, he was an ALL-NFL selection.

The superior running game of the Miami Dolphins was again too much for teams to handle in 1973. Csonka lugged the ball for 1003 yards and an average of 4.6 yards per carry. The Dolphins lost only two games that year and again won the Super Bowl, defeating the Minnesota Vikings, 24-7. Gaining 145 yards in 33 carries and scoring two touchdowns, "Zonk" was named the Most Valuable Player in Super Bowl VIII. In addition, he was selected as the Super Athlete of the Year by the Pro Football Writers of America.

Playing out his option with Miami, Larry Csonka—along with his Dolphin teammates Jim Kiick and Paul Warfield—signed a multi-year contract with the Memphis Southmen of the new World Football League (WFL). After playing only one season (1975) in the WFL, the league folded. Csonka became a free agent and was signed by the New York Giants of the NFL in 1976. He became the highest-salaried Giant in the team's history.

He rejoined the Miami Dolphins before the 1979 season, but many doubted whether Larry could regain his top form. He surprised everyone with a great year. He rushed for 837 yards and 12

touchdowns, and helped lead Miami to a divisional title.

Csonka retired in 1980 with 8081 career rushing yards. The total placed him sixth among the NFL's all-time leading ground-gainers. In 1987, Larry Csonka was inducted into the Pro Football Hall of Fame.

Lawrence Richard Csonka was born on Christmas Day, 1946, in Stow, Ohio. His family later moved to a farm, where Larry Csonka grew up. At Stow High School, he starred in football, track, and wrestling.

At Syracuse, Csonka played the first three games of his sophomore year as a linebacker before coach Schwartzwalder moved him to the fullback position. In his senior year, Csonka once carried four tacklers on his back for 14 yards. In close games, he proved himself the dependable workhorse of his team. Against Maryland, he carried the ball 43 times during the game.

As the number-one draft choice of the Miami Dolphins in 1968, Larry Csonka received $100,000 for signing. It was a bargain for Miami, for probably no other player turned out to be so dedicated. Without Csonka, there might have been no winning streak to make football history for the Dolphins, when they finished the 1972-1973 season without a single loss.